BETH OPPENHEIMER

Enchantment of the World

ARGENTINA

by Martin Hintz

Consultant: George I. Blanksten, Ph.D., Professor of Political Science, Northwestern University

Consultant for Reading: Robert L. Hillerich, Ph.D., Bowling Green State University, Bowling Green, Ohio

CHILDRENS PRESS ®

CHICAGO

Ushuaia, at the southern tip of South America, is called the southernmost city in the world. The weather is chilly year-round and the mountains are usually covered with snow.

For assistance in preparing *Enchantment of the World: Argentina*, the author would like to thank the cultural affairs division of the Argentine embassy and the Argentine ministries of economics, press relations and culture, education, and interior.

Library of Congress Cataloging in Publication Data

Hintz, Martin.
  Argentina.

  (Enchantment of the world)
  Includes index.
  Summary: An introduction to the history, geography, economics, customs, and people of the eighth largest nation in the world.
  1. Argentina—Juvenile literature. [1. Argentina]
I. Title. II. Series.
F2808.2.H56 1985   982   85-2638
ISBN 0-516-02752-2   AACR2

EIGHTH PRINTING, 1994.

Picture Acknowledgments
Chip and Rosa Maria Peterson: Pages 4, 6 (bottom), 8, 14 (bottom), 18, 54 (bottom), 64, 65, 67 (bottom), 68 (bottom), 72 (left), 73, 74, 109
© **Victor Englebert:** Pages 5, 11 (bottom), 19, 85 (left), 96 (top), 98, 106
© **Stuart Cohen:** Pages 6 (top), 12, 17, 36, 58 (bottom), 59 (top), 60 (2 photos), 62, 99, 101, 104
Nawrocki Stock Photo: © Mark Stevenson: Pages 11 (top), 54 (top), 68 (top), 72 (right), 77; © Mark Gamba: Cover, Pages 14 (top), 67 (top); © Ruth Dunbar: Pages 88, 89
Root Resources: © Kenneth W. Fink: Page 21 (bottom left); © Lois M. Kransz: Page 23 (2 photos)
Stock Imagery: © Fairchild: Pages 13, 24 (top), 29, 35, 39, 40, 41, 43, 44, 45, 56, 63, 79, 80, 82 (left), 85 (right), 91, 108 (bottom)
Tom Stack & Associates: © Gary Milburn: Page 21 (top left); © Fiona Sunquist: Page 21 (top right); © Warren Garst: 21 (bottom right)
Historical Pictures Service, Chicago: Pages 24 (bottom), 26, 27 (left), 32, 33, 34, 42, 46, 51
Roloc Color Slides: Pages 9, 27 (right), 70
United Press International: Pages 47, 49, 50, 52, 81, 86
Cameramann International: Pages 58 (top), 59 (bottom), 61, 71, 87, 96 (bottom), 100, 102, 108 (top)
Hillstrom Stock Photo: © Victor Banks: Pages 75, 78, 82 (right)
Associated Press/Wide World: Pages 93, 95
© **Virginia Grimes:** Page 105
Len W. Meents: Maps on pages 19, 62, 65, 67
Courtesy Flag Research Center, Winchester, Massachusetts 01890: Flag on back cover
Cover: Hotel Llao-Llao in the Andes

Youngsters on the pampa, where cattle raising is the main industry, practice using a lasso.

TABLE OF CONTENTS

More than one third of the people live in the metropolitan area of Buenos Aires (above) and many areas, such as Chubut Province in Patagonia (below), are sparsely populated.

Chapter 1

LOOKING AT ARGENTINA

How to describe Argentina? There are several ways. Tell of the immense size of the country: Argentina is the eighth-largest nation in the world, the fourth-largest in the Americas, and the second-largest in South America. Talk about the Argentines: hardworking, industrious, forward-looking. Then there's the wealth of Argentina: minerals, agriculture, livestock, scenery.

Despite all these exciting attributes, Argentina still has problems. Since the 1930s, its political history has been tumultuous. Dictators and military coups have left their mark. The 1980s have not been pleasant for the country. Economically once powerful, Argentina owes a great deal of money to banks elsewhere in the world because it borrowed so much in previous years.

But Argentina is working on these difficulties and with luck will eventually overcome them. The Argentines are a proud people. They have faced other problems in their long and colorful

An arm of the Río de la Plata, called the Riachuelo,
is used as a freight dock and a fishing port of Buenos Aires.

history. They have always managed to work themselves out of
what might seem to be terrible situations. The country has always
become stronger as a result.

No country ever stands still. It goes through trying times and
happy times. If its people are willing and eager to work together
and if they respect the views and attitudes of their neighbors, they
have a good chance of solving their problems.

GEOGRAPHICAL LINKS

Argentina is linked to Uruguay and Paraguay by the river Plata.
This water system is actually several rivers that eventually flow
into the Atlantic Ocean at Buenos Aires, the capital of Argentina.
The Plata includes the Pilcomayo River, which flows into the
Paraguay River and makes up much of the border between
Argentina and Paraguay. The Paraná River flows out of Brazil to
the north, along the eastern border of Paraguay. The Paraguay

Rugged peaks of the Andes along the Chile-Argentina border

River eventually joins the Paraná. The Uruguay River starts in the same general area as the Paraná, but makes up the border between Uruguay and Argentina, flowing southward to the mouth of the Plata in Argentina.

A broad estuary, where an ocean meets a river, was one of the first places in the New World discovered by Spanish explorers. They named this wide bay the Río de la Plata—not knowing at the time that the estuary was really made up of several rivers. The banks are so wide that one cannot see across from the Argentina side to the Uruguay shore.

Linking Argentina to Chile on the west and to Bolivia on the north are the high crags of the Andes Mountains. The mountains form natural borders.

Using geography is an abstract way to describe Argentina. The Plata River system and the Andes are examples of how one nation can be joined naturally to its neighbors. But the size of the peaks and the width of the water also serve to keep the bordering nations separate.

Of course, there are many more obvious reasons why the Argentines are a special people. Any nationality is special in its own way. It is important to note, however, that there is less disparity between Argentina's wealthy people and its poor classes than in some other Latin American countries. There is a large middle class in Argentina, made up of shopkeepers, mechanics, teachers, service workers, and many others. Almost everyone in Argentina can read and write, a feature unmatched by some larger nations.

There isn't much racial strife. Most of the people are basically of European stock. The Spaniards and Italians are the two largest ethnic groups, followed closely by British, German, Swiss, Jewish, Arabic, Oriental, and Slavic nationalities. For the most part, everyone gets along fairly well. Immigration was very important in building up the country. Argentina has been lucky to have the skills and talents of all these people.

CITY VS. COUNTRYSIDE

If there are any intra-Argentine differences, they are most obvious between city dwellers and those who live in the countryside. Today, about four-fifths of the Argentines live in cities or larger towns. Many residents of the huge metropolis of Buenos Aires feel that their city is all that is important to Argentina. More than one third of the entire country lives in the capital or its suburbs.

Of course, this makes the folks in smaller towns and the farmers very unhappy. This divisive quality has often led to political

Life for the people in the capital city of Buenos Aires (above)
is very different from life on the pampa (below).

Wealthy plantation owners sometimes live in Spanish colonial haciendas.

unrest. It was a problem even before Argentina became independent. The people of Buenos Aires, called *porteños* (people of the port), battled the *caudillos* (the rich landowners from the provinces) for power.

Argentine society has been influenced by this history. As the port cities grew rich and strong, the poorer people from the provinces flocked to the coast to find work. Often they had trouble landing jobs because they were unskilled. These unemployed were called "the shirtless ones." They often supported dictators who promised them a better life.

The upper and middle classes in the cities feared these newcomers and distrusted politicians. On occasion, the military stepped in to run things because it felt it could do a better job than the quarreling civilians.

*A proud grandmother and her grandson smile as she
holds a photo of them taken when they were much younger.*

Despite these differences, Argentines are fairly close-knit.
Families are extremely important, with loyalty considered a great
virtue. Family connections are often necessary to get a good job or
even to get into a good school. The family is always there to help.

This quality is both a strength and a weakness for Argentina.
Depending too much on a close circle can restrict one's vision. But
it also makes for a powerful force that can withstand turmoil from
the outside.

So there you have it: Argentina. Confusing, perhaps, if you take
only a quick look. But on closer inspection, certainly an
enchanting nation.

Contrasting climates can be found in Argentina. There are ice caps in Patagonia near Antarctica (above) and low mountains and desert valleys (below) east of the Andes in San Juan Province.

Chapter 2

THE WEDGE-SHAPED LAND

Few countries can match Argentina's differences in climate and landscape. Border disputes with its neighbors have caused many different figures regarding Argentina's size to appear in record books. Official government statistics indicate that Argentina's South American landmass is 1,073,400 square miles (2,780,092 square kilometers). Argentina and Great Britain both claim the South Georgia, South Sandwich, and South Orkney islands and the Malvinas (or Falkland) Islands. In 1982, the two countries went to war over who owned the Malvinas.

As an example of this territorial confusion, consider the Malvinas, windswept hunks of rock suitable primarily for sheep raising. In 1592, the islands were discovered by English explorer John Davis. The French and Spaniards also claimed the Malvinas at various times. When the Spaniards were deposed, the Argentine government claimed the islands in 1820. But Argentina was not strong enough to keep them. In 1833, the British retook the islands. They continued to hold title through the mid-1980s.

But in 1982 the military rulers of Argentina decided the British occupation was an insult to their national dignity. So they invaded and captured the Malvinas. Yet after several months of land and sea battles, the British pushed the Argentines off the islands.

HOT, COLD, AND BIG

Mainland Argentina is big. One quarter of Europe would fit within the recognized boundaries of Argentina. It is six times larger than Spain! And that doesn't include another vast chunk of territory in Antarctica that Argentina claims—(374,300 square miles-969,464 square kilometers)—all frostbitten.

Argentina stretches some 2,300 miles (3,700 kilometers) from its wide northern borders to the skinny tip of Tierra del Fuego on the south. Tierra del Fuego, which means "Land of Fire," is a small island shared with Chile.

Shaped like a blunted wedge, Argentina is 980 miles (1,577 kilometers) wide at its widest point, but averages about 466 miles (750 kilometers) wide. The country abruptly ends in the rough waters of the Beagle Channel, which separates Tierra del Fuego from some smaller islands owned by Chile.

Argentina's 2,940 miles (4,731 kilometers) of Atlantic coastline—its eastern frontier—differ sharply from the Andes Mountains on the west. In between is enough variety of landscape and temperature to satisfy any traveler. The heat can be intense in the north, just as intense as the cold in the far south. But generally, Argentina's climate is temperate. Its seasons are the reverse of those in the Northern Hemisphere. Summer in Europe and the United States occurs during winter in Argentina.

Gauchos working on a ranch on the pampa

PAMPA AND PEAKS

Argentina can easily be divided into three major sections. First, there are the pampa—the flat, fertile plains in the east central section. Soil there is fine sand, clay, and dirt washed eastward by wind and rainstorms that sweep over the land.

Hardly a single rock rises very high in that entire region, except for some low hills near Mar del Plata on the Atlantic coast and some very old mountains in central Argentina. The pampa are now crisscrossed by rail lines and highways, but in the old days they were similar to the Wild West in the United States. Thousands of cattle used to roam the open range, herded by Argentina's national folk heroes, the gauchos, the South American cowboys.

A view of the Chilean section of the road across the Andes connecting Los Andes, Chile and Mendoza, Argentina

The pampa cover more than 250,959 square miles (650,000 square kilometers).

Along the wild, western boundaries of Argentina are the rugged Andes Mountains, the world's second-highest peaks. They run like a spine along the whole length of South America. Some of the peaks are as high as 19,000 feet (5,791 meters). The highest mountain in the Western Hemisphere is in Argentina. This is Mount Aconcagua, at 22,831 feet (6,959 meters).

Many deep valleys scar the mountains. Some of the wider valleys are called *quebradas*. Since the days of Spanish rule, the *quebradas* have been used as transportation routes across the Andes. The Uspallata Pass, at 12,600 feet (3,840 meters), is one of the main routes to Chile. The Spanish explorers named it the *Camino de los Andes,* the Road of the Andes.

During the revolutionary wars of the 1800s, when all of South America was rebelling against Spain, the *Camino de los Andes* was

Valdés Península in Patagonia juts out into the Atlantic Ocean.

very important. Many armies marched back and forth through this cut in the mountains. Now a railroad makes travel a little easier. Even small airplanes use the pass, rather than attempt to fly over the higher portions of the Andes.

But travel still is not easy. In the winter, terrible snowstorms rage between the steep valley walls. The passes are often blocked by deep drifts.

PATAGONIA: WIDE AND RUGGED

In the south and east of the mountains, rolling hills blend into broad plains. This region, called Patagonia, comprises about one quarter of Argentina. The wide, rugged area is crisscrossed by deep canyons.

In the rainy season, these canyons are filled with rushing, muddy floodwater. In the hot summer, the canyons are empty. It is often very foggy and chilly in Patagonia. The land, not suitable for farming, is used for raising sheep. Only cactuses and stunted trees grow very well.

Between 1910 and 1921, the government built some irrigation canals along the Río Negro, a major river in Patagonia. This allowed orchards and vineyards to be developed. By now, this portion of Patagonia is valuable, since tons of grapes and other fruit are produced every year.

However, since the rest of Patagonia is so uncomfortable, only about 3 percent of Argentina's population lives there. Although not many people are around, there are many wild animals. The Patagonian gray fox, a mouse-sized opossum, and the hairy armadillo are rare elsewhere but are plentiful in Patagonia. There are numerous exotic birds, such as the tufted tit-tyrant, the crested tinamou, the rhea, and the red-backed hawk.

Patagonia extends to the Atlantic shoreline. Sea lions, dolphins, penguins, and seabirds are everywhere. Killer whales feed on these creatures.

MESOPOTAMIA AND THE CHACO

Northern Argentina is divided into the Chaco and Mesopotamia. The first area is just east of the Andes. The second lies between the Paraná and Uruguay rivers. It reminded early pioneers of the fertile land in present-day Iraq between the Euphrates and the Tigris rivers, which also was called Mesopotamia.

The Chaco extends into Paraguay, western Brazil, and eastern

Some of the animals living in Argentina are (clockwise from above left):
armadillos, opossums, jaguars, and penguins.

Bolivia. It is a great plain, with many rivers. Houses near the rivers are raised on log piles or placed on earth embankments because of the many spring floods. Despite the heavy rainfall, irrigation is necessary for the crops. The hot weather in the Chaco causes the water to evaporate quickly.

An interesting tree grows in the Chaco. It is the *quebracho*, nicknamed the "ax-breaker" because its wood is so hard. For that reason, the wood is valuable for use as railroad ties, fence posts, and telephone poles. It is also a source of tannin, a substance used in tanning leather. Over the years, woodcutters have devastated much of the *quebracho* forests, which have not been replanted. It takes more than one hundred years for a *quebracho* to mature, so there are fewer and fewer of these strange trees remaining in Argentina. Cotton is now being grown where the trees used to stand.

Mesopotamia has plenty of rain, making it a fine agricultural region. There are many swamps and forests. Some portions of Mesopotamia are tropical. Monkeys, jaguars, and wild hogs roam the dense jungles. Brilliantly colored parrots, hummingbirds, and toucans flit from tree to tree.

The Iguaçu River, which Argentina shares with Brazil, tumbles into a waterfall that is larger than Niagara Falls on the United States-Canadian border. For a distance of about three miles (five kilometers), the water tumbles and roars over jagged rocks. It then pours over a precipice.

Jesuit missionaries settled in the area in the 1500s, cultivating a plant called *yerba maté*. From this, they made a bitter herbal tea that is still a popular drink. The priests set up a string of missions throughout Mesopotamia, which were havens for Indians fleeing slave traders. The Indians often got their revenge, however, on the

The magnificent Iguaçu Falls, 8,100 feet (2,469 meters) wide with drops of 200 feet (61 meters) are in the forests of the north on the Argentina-Brazil border. Visitors can get close through a system of catwalks that wind along the edge of the Paraná River and skirt the falls.

slavers. Headhunters were once common in the region. More than one trader literally "lost his head" on an expedition. There even used to be a headshrinkers museum in Dos de Mayo, a village near Posadas, the capital of the province of Misiones.

The town of Paraná in Mesopotamia was once the capital of the Argentine Confederation. Currently, there are twenty-three provinces in Argentina, with the capital now being Buenos Aires. The city is its own federal district. Several offshore islands are considered to be a national territory.

All in all, Argentina takes up almost one quarter of South America. The train from Buenos Aires to the town of San Salvador de Jujuy in northwest Argentina makes a journey of 1,000 miles (1,609 kilometers). From Buenos Aires south to the port of Río Gallegos is almost 1,600 miles (2,574 kilometers).

Above: Many Indians live in Jujuy Province, near the Bolivian border.
Below: Most Argentine gauchos are mestizos, *people of mixed Indian and European ancestry.*

Chapter 3

A COLONY OF SILVER

Indians were living in Argentina a thousand years before the first whites ever dreamed of venturing away from Europe. There were at least twenty major tribes and numerous subgroups who lived in the pampa, the mountains, and along the sea. They were basically nomads, who lived by hunting. Those who lived in the mountain valleys were more advanced. They had permanent towns, terraced fields, and an extensive trading system.

Most of the Argentine Indians were more primitive than the urban-oriented Inca, Maya, and Aztec of Peru, Bolivia, and Mexico. The Argentine Indians were great hunters. They would chase herds of deer for days, without letting the animals eat or drink. Eventually, the deer became exhausted and were easily killed by arrows and rocks flung from slings.

A favorite Indian weapon was the *boleadoras.* Two or three stones were tied together by leather thongs. They could be thrown accurately up to 100 yards (91 meters), wrapping around the legs of an animal and tripping it.

An early drawing of Patagonian Indians

Instead of growing wheat, tribes such as the Querandi would make a "flour" mash of crushed and roasted locusts! Most Indians dressed in skins or furs.

EXPLORERS AND "SAVAGES"

The first European explorers were not impressed. They considered all the Indians to be nothing but savages. They wanted to use the tribes as laborers. They didn't realize that there were many differences between such tribes as the Guarani, Huarpes, Comechingones, and others. The Spaniards saw only hunting Indians and the few settled Indians. They haughtily made fun of the tribes, calling them "grease eaters" because many Indians ate animal fats.

This proved to be a big error on the part of the colonizers. When the warlike Araucanians invaded Argentina from Chile, the Spaniards weren't prepared. Bands of one hundred to two

Ferdinand Magellan (left) discovered the strait at the bottom of South America that now bears his name and used it as a corridor between the Pacific and Atlantic oceans. An Araucanian Indian woman (right), reported to be over one hundred years old, spins wool.

hundred mounted warriors swooped down on their villages and missions. Many early Argentine towns were destroyed by the brave marauders.

The Araucanians eventually controlled most of Patagonia and a great deal of the pampa. They tamed the horses turned loose on the pampa by the Spaniards and used them for cavalry. Much like the Plains Indians of North America, they lived by raiding. Captured cattle would be driven over the Andes to be traded with the Araucanians' Chilean relatives.

The wandering Araucanians weren't defeated until the end of the 1800s, when the railroads were pushed through the pampa.

Early in the 1500s the explorer Ferdinand Magellan encountered Indians at the tip of South America. He thought they had very big feet. He wrote long tales about the giants in the terrible lands of Patagonia.

The peaceful Indians were not giants. But they were taller than the average Spaniard or Portuguese. As such, they looked very frightening. They hunted seals, guanaco, and rhea. Eventually, later explorers realized these hardy, outdoor people would not bother them.

The first Spaniard to land in what is now Argentina was Juan Díaz de Solís. He had been told by the king of Spain to find a passage to the Pacific Ocean around South America. Díaz de Solís found the mouth of the Río de la Plata, the River of Silver. Today, the river flows past Argentina's capital of Buenos Aires. But in 1516, only grassy plains edged its shores. Díaz de Solís decided to explore upstream.

Taking a squad of soldiers and sailors from his main ship, Díaz de Solís rowed ashore in a small boat when he saw some Indians who looked friendly. The Spaniards were invited to dinner. They didn't realize that they would be the main course. The Indians ate them. So much for the first European arrivals!

But some of Díaz de Solís's men survived. The lucky ones eventually made it back to Spain. They carried trinkets of silver that friendlier Indians had given them. This launched a silver rush to Argentina.

In fact, the word *argentina* means "silver" or "silvery" in Spanish. It came from the Latin term for silver, *argentum.* Thus the nation of Argentina is the Silver Country.

But the fortune hunters were disappointed. They found little silver along the coast and soon gave up. For many years afterward, it was easier to cross the Andes from the Bolivian and Chilean side of the mountains. That's where the Indians had their silver mines. In addition, the Spaniards had to contend with Portuguese who were colonizing Brazil, just up the coast from Argentina. Spain didn't want a war so far from home.

A painting showing Pedro de Mendoza and his men arriving in Buenos Aires.

THE BIRTH OF BUENOS AIRES

To solidify their hold on Argentina, the Spaniards built a fort on the southern shore of the Río de la Plata in 1536. Pedro de Mendoza brought fifteen hundred men with him to set up the base, which was called Buenos Aires. The tiny settlement was constantly attacked by the Querandi Indians, so the Spaniards moved across the river to what is now Paraguay.

There they founded the city of Asunción. From there, they sent out parties to colonize the interior of Argentina. In 1580, some brave adventurers from Asunción returned and rebuilt the fort at Buenos Aires.

It remained a small town for generations, simply a center for breeding mules. Most of the attention of the Spaniards was focused on territories farther north. Goods were hauled by mule from the pampa, over trails made by the Inca across the Andes, to the power centers of Lima, Peru, and Mexico City. From there, the Spaniards took the treasures across Panama in Central America. There they were loaded on galleons for shipment to Spain. Nobody thought much about what was going on in Argentina.

THE JOKE OF SMUGGLING

This ignoring of Argentina contributed to the independent spirit of the few Spaniards who remained on the fringe of Spain's New World empire. Their descendants had to be rough and rugged to survive. One of the principal occupations became smuggling. It was hard for the Spanish authorities, called viceroys, to control Argentina because it was so far away from the ruling country.

Negro slaves from Africa, tallow, hides, wool, horns, and crops all would disappear along the trade routes from the pampa. The goods were to be delivered to Lima, but very few actually made it there. Many villages were established at trade route crossroads during those years. Sante Fe, Córdoba, Catamarca, Santiago del Estero, Tucumán, Salta, and Jujuy all became rich and thriving.

Some of the most prosperous citizens got their start with illegally obtained supplies. Smuggling was considered a good joke to play on the stuffy Spanish governors "from up north."

By the 1700s, the Spanish policy changed. In 1778, a free trade policy opened up the entire Atlantic coast. This meant a boom for Buenos Aires. Goods could be shipped directly to Spain from the growing city. Merchants grew wealthy.

By this time, the people of Argentina were no longer pure Spanish. There were large numbers of Creoles, or *Criollos,* as they were sometimes called. They were the children of European-born parents. But eventually, even the Creole bloodlines became hazy, although they made up the wealthy power structure in the towns. The lower classes were called *mestizos,* Europeans with mixed Indian background. Many immigrants from Germany, Holland, and Italy also arrived. The face of Argentina was changing.

Eventually the Andean silver mines ran dry and commerce slowed, but the king of Spain wanted still more money from his South American colonies. So he sold huge tracts of land to the Creoles. Sometimes, a single land sale involved a million acres (404,700 hectares).

The Spaniards subdivided their empire in a vain attempt to protect their interests from the Portuguese and the English. A new viceroyalty of the Río de la Plata was set up. Buenos Aires was made its capital. Immediately, trouble developed.

A TASTE OF INDEPENDENCE

The Creoles were used to running things their way. But the king sent many bureaucrats from Spain to administer the newly formed territory. Royal clerks, judges, military officers, and others looked down on the native Argentines. It didn't help that the newcomers tried to enforce tax laws.

The situation in the 1790s was similar to that of the American colonies twenty years earlier. The wealthy Creole merchant class, the bankers, the local politicians, and the big landowners wanted independence. They approved of the American and French revolutions. We can do the same thing, they told each other.

The English staged a surprise attack on Argentina in 1806.

The English watched this with interest, although they were still upset about losing their own American colonies. But they needed a trade outlet and looked on South American markets as a good source of money. Only Spain stood in the way.

Although Argentina was a long way from Europe, both in distance and temperament, the country was soon swept up in the revolutionary wars sweeping its mother continent. The French under Napoleon Bonaparte were making vassal states out of many European nations and threatening others, including Spain. The English, who were battling the French, saw an opportunity to gain some economic and political advantages in South America. In 1806, the English attacked Argentina, figuring that Spain was too occupied in Europe to offer much help to its colony. The gamble paid off.

*General
William Carr
Beresford*

The officials in Buenos Aires were taken by surprise. On June 27, the city was taken over by the veteran Highland Seventy-first Regiment, a contingent of artillerymen and seven dragoons. Their commander, General William Carr Beresford, had just captured Cape Town, South Africa, from the Dutch. He was considered a military hero, especially since much treasure was sent back to England to show that Argentina was a wealthy prize.

But the people of Buenos Aires didn't like the English any better than they liked the Spaniards. In August of that same year, the townspeople revolted. They quickly captured all the English and Scottish soldiers and sent them to prison in the interior. Argentines proudly remember that time, calling it the *Reconquista*.

Much later, in a twist of history, the British embassy in Argentina was located for a time on a Buenos Aires street called the Calle Reconquista.

The first permanent settlement of Buenos Aires, with its natural harbor, was in 1580.

The Argentines refused to let the Spanish viceroy return to power. They had tasted independence.

A VICTORY AND A REBELLION

The British were angry because some of their best soldiers were captured by forces they considered to be only ragtag city folk. They mounted another offensive. On July 5, 1807, more British landed at Buenos Aires. They met the same fate. The people fired on the enemy from the housetops, from doorways, and from barricades across the streets. They even threw chamber pots down on the heads of the poor soldiers. In one day, the British army lost four hundred men killed and hundreds wounded.

The unhappy British commander hurriedly signed a treaty with Santiago Liniers, a Frenchman who had served in the Spanish army. He had been named "viceroy" by the people of Buenos

*The influence of the British settlers can be seen
in this half-timbered house in Mar del Plata.*

Aires for his help in defending the city in the first British
invasion.

This second victory over the British was called the *Defensa*.

It showed that the Argentines could defend their claims that
they could take care of themselves. No longer did they need
Spain's assistance.

This attitude was reinforced in 1808, when the armies of
France's Napoleon Bonaparte invaded Spain and deposed the king
there. Joseph Bonaparte, Napoleon's brother, was installed as
Spain's ruler. Back in Argentina, the people of Buenos Aires
rebelled against the Spanish viceroy in 1810. He had been sent to
replace Liniers after the British were defeated. Nobody liked the
fellow anyway and the French invasion of Spain was a good
excuse for dumping him.

On May 25, 1810, the Creoles formed their own government in
Buenos Aires. From that day, the Argentines mark the start of
their journey to total independence.

A statue of General José de San Martín, the liberator of Argentina, dominates the Plaza San Martín in Buenos Aires.

Chapter 4

ONGOING REVOLUTION

The Creoles who formed the new Argentine government had no love for France. They nominally supported the deposed Spanish king, Ferdinand VII, saying they simply didn't like the representatives he sent to Argentina. They also realized that they would need trade with the outside world, even with England, to ensure their hard-won freedom.

They had seen how business improved when the English controlled Buenos Aires. Everyone had been able to purchase inexpensive goods. All trade restrictions imposed by the Spanish had been dropped, making the merchants very happy. They were pragmatic about their politics. When the English eventually allied themselves with the deposed Spanish king, this gave the Argentines an excuse to rebel against the French as well. They certainly didn't like any outside rulers.

What complicated everything was the fact that few towns in the interior had been invited to join in the overthrow of the Spanish viceroy. Many people still had a warm feeling for the country of Spain, if not for its government.

This was one factor that led to a long-standing split between Buenos Aires and the rest of the country. Even today, there is some bitterness between the countryside and the capital.

Most towns of the interior were still held by the Spanish army loyal to Ferdinand, if not to the French-supported king. A lot of Argentines were not ready to sever their ties to Spain.

It was a very confusing era.

A WAR OF INDEPENDENCE

Although they continued to claim support of Ferdinand, the Creole leaders in Buenos Aires decided to rid the country of all Spanish troops and others who opposed their rebellion. In fact, former viceroy Santiago Liniers was arrested and executed. After he had been replaced as ruler in Buenos Aires, he had rejoined the Spanish forces. In the eyes of his former friends, that was unforgivable.

On November 7, 1810, the patriots, as they were called in Buenos Aires, defeated a Spanish army at Suipacha. This was the first victory of a totally Argentine force over an outside enemy. The fighting had become a war of independence.

The rebels were not totally successful, although they had excellent military commanders, such as Manuel Belgrano and Mariano Moreno. The governments in Buenos Aires kept changing. They failed to keep control of much of the Andes. A hugh chunk of Argentine territory eventually came under Bolivian authority. Neighboring Paraguay did not join their revolution.

Manuel Belgrano, one of the revolutionary leaders

The people in the interior were prevented from trading with anyone except the *porteños*, the people of the port—Buenos Aires. For years, they had struggled against this economic domination. They felt it was as heavy as the Spaniards' political domination. In addition, Buenos Aires claimed to be the ruling center of any new national government. No one else was given the chance to complain, petition, or otherwise be heard.

The Spaniards continually threatened to march back into Argentina from their strongholds in Chile and Peru. General José de San Martín, one of Argentina's most able patriot generals, saw that it was important to attack the Spaniards on their home ground.

José de San Martín is considered Argentina's greatest hero.

San Martín invaded Chile, leading his army through the Los Patos and Uspallata passes in the Andes. Under his leadership, Chile was captured and he went on to take Peru. Spain's power in South America was broken by the mid-1800s.

FREEDOM, BUT NO PEACE

At this time, Argentina was called the Provinces of the Río de la Plata. On July 9, 1816, an official proclamation of independence had been made. The Argentines finally considered themselves free of any foreign control. However, many of the delegates to an independence conference favored having their own king. The country was not at peace. A succession of juntas, triumvirates, and

Bernardino Rivadavia was the first president of Argentina.

supreme directors tried to consolidate control. Nothing worked.

Each provincial city wanted to be independent. A congress under the control of Buenos Aires factions attempted to write a constitution in 1819. It stated that central authority should be located in their city. Of course, the *caudillos,* the provincial leaders, shouted down that idea.

Anarchy was the order of the day. In one year, 1820, Buenos Aires had twenty-four governors! Civil war broke out between the *federales,* those from the interior who wished to keep their local independence, and the *unitarios,* those who wanted a central government.

In 1826, Bernardino Rivadavia, a highly respected Argentine, was elected president. This briefly halted the bloodshed. Rivadavia

Secret police spying and violent actions against the Indians of the pampa were common during the dictatorial rule of Juan Manuel de Rosas.

encouraged immigration and introduced many reforms in government, finance, and education. But he couldn't please everyone. Both the *unitarios* and the *federales* were afraid of him. So he was deposed and civil war broke out again. Manuel Dorrego, a federalist, was the next president. He was generally unpopular and was assassinated.

STRONG MEN AND SIEGES

In 1828, Juan Manuel de Rosas became leader of the *federales*. He was a strong man who had a great deal of support from the gauchos. He allowed no one to challenge his rule. His secret police were very efficient and many *unitarios* disappeared under strange

After leading the revolt against Rosas, Justo José de Urquiza was elected president in 1853.

circumstances. Exile was best for anyone wanting to get away from Rosas.

Rosas closed the Paraná and Paraguay rivers to outside commerce. He wanted his own business interests to make all the profits. The French objected to this tactic and blockaded Buenos Aires in 1838. Rosas was able to repel them and kept up his restrictive trade practices. So in 1848, a combined French and English fleet returned, hoping to break Rosas's power. The Argentines finally drove them away after a long siege of Buenos Aires. By this time, the Argentine people had had enough of Rosas. In 1852 he was finally overthrown by Justo José de Urquiza, one of his former aides.

Bartolomé Mitre, the third president of Argentina, worked at stabilizing the government.

After Rosas was deposed, a constitutional convention met in 1853. The Argentines wrote a document that is still in effect. It granted a great deal more power to the president than does the United States Constitution. One important but controversial provision enables the Argentine president to suspend constitutional guarantees if he considers the country to be "under siege." This means the president can take over many governmental powers that would ordinarily belong to Congress or the courts. Unfortunately, this clause has been used frequently in Argentine history.

WARS, INDIANS, AND BORDERS

The Province of Buenos Aires broke away from the Argentine Confederation because it didn't like Urquiza's government. The

Domingo Sarmiento was interested in improving public education in Argentina.

porteños didn't think he cared about their problems. In 1859, war erupted between the province and the rest of the country.

In 1861, the troops from Buenos Aires won a decisive victory under the leadership of General Bartolomé Mitre. The country was reunited and Buenos Aires again became the capital.

The next three presidents, Mitre, Domingo Faustino Sarmiento, and Nicola Avellenda, all were intellectuals who favored better education for the people. They also supported more immigration. But their administrations had a dark side as well. Under their rule, the Indians were finally defeated in Patagonia. The Araucanians could not compete with an army that carried repeating rifles. This was called the Conquest of the Desert. It opened new lands for immigrants and native Argentines. But the Indian culture was destroyed. Hardly any trace remains.

In 1865, Argentina fought a border war with Paraguay. Allied

In 1892, a meeting of the Unión Cívica Radical *ran into conflict with the police of Buenos Aires.*

with Brazil and Uruguay, Argentine troops defeated the smaller nation. The conflict was nicknamed the War of the Triple Alliance. It was a horror for everyone concerned. The Paraguayans fought to the death. Almost every adult male in the country was killed.

Argentina slowly was consolidated. The pampa were fenced in, industry expanded, and many gauchos moved into the city slums when their ranch jobs ended. The economy boomed, helped in large part by English investments. A growing middle class demanded more political power.

REFORM, FOR A WHILE

The *Unión Cívica Radical,* or Radical party, grew strong. It sought a universal secret ballot for all Argentine men. In the old

A 1930 photo of Hipólito Irigoyen, president from 1916 to 1922 and again from 1928 until he was overthrown in 1930

days, only the landowners and wealthy could vote. In 1910, Roque Sáenz Peña was inaugurated as president. He favored relaxed voting rules and with his help, Congress passed such laws. In 1916, Hipólito Irigoyen was the first Argentine elected under the reforms.

But Irigoyen was not a good president. He never seemed to know what to do and his goverment was corrupt. He was well liked as a person, but not as president. He left office in disgrace in 1922. The next president, Marcelo T. de Alvear, did not last long either. The political parties looked for candidates to succeed Alvear. Irigoyen made a comeback. He was still popular enough to be reelected in 1928. He was almost eighty years old.

Again Irigoyen seemed to keep stumbling over himself. The

Great Depression, a financial crisis that shook the world, smashed hard into Argentina. Businesses collapsed, banks were ruined, people panicked. The army revolted on September 6, 1930, ousting Irigoyen and launching a succession of military governments, which ended for the most part in 1983, with the election of civilian president Dr. Raúl Alfonsín.

The general who finally emerged as Argentine leader was José F. Uriburu, an extreme conservative. He declared a state of siege but was forced to call for elections and was defeated. Several other presidents followed quickly after Uriburu in unstable times.

During World War II, the leaders of the army favored Nazi Germany and Fascist Italy. Argentina always had strong ties to Germany and many of their officers had been trained there. The military expected the Nazis to win the war and supported pro-German activities throughout South America.

They didn't believe that President Ramón S. Castillo would keep Argentina neutral in the war. They thought he might support the large English community then living in Argentina. So the military rebelled again in 1943.

THE TIMES OF PERÓNS

The new regime arrested many labor leaders and liberals. This upset most Argentines. They demanded that the repression stop. Seizing on this attitude was Juan Perón, a young officer who had served in several governmental positions over the years. He had the foresight to build a strong following among the workers. The military arrested Perón but freed him when thousands of his supporters marched to Buenos Aires to demand that he become a candidate for president.

Juan Perón and his wife Eva (Evita) drive through Buenos Aires in July, 1952, just before the death of Eva.

Perón was elected president in 1946 and his Labor party controlled Congress. He ruled for the next nine years, supporting what he considered to be industrial and agricultural reforms. However, Perón grew increasingly more dictatorial. With the help of María Eva Duarte Perón, his second wife, he removed from office all the labor leaders who once had supported him. It was said that Eva, nicknamed Evita, was the real power behind Perón.

The Peronistas, the followers of Perón, shut down opposition newspapers and magazines, restricted political parties, and wrote their own constitution. The Peróns remained popular, however. Eva gave a lot of money to the poor and snubbed the rich people. But she was very vindictive. Anybody who questioned her motives got into trouble. Many people were jailed.

HOMENAJE A EVA PERON

Holding lighted candles, Argentines mourn the death of Eva Perón.

Eva Perón died in 1952. There was national mourning after her death. She had been well liked despite her governmental abuses. (A prizewinning British musical called *Evita,* later a success elsewhere, was modeled after her life.)

Eventually, Perón lost the support of the Catholic church. Some of his more radical followers attacked and beat priests who protested the government's treatment of its opponents. Several churches were burned. However, many of Perón's more moderate followers were good Catholics. They became disillusioned with his activities and his growing dislike of the church. They didn't like the controversy that was growing in Argentina. Neither did the military.

The navy and air force attempted a coup in June, 1955, but it failed. They tried again—"successfully"—in September of that

Arturo Frondizi became president in 1958. He was overthrown in 1962.

year, with the added support of the army and numerous armed civilians. Perón fled into exile, eventually finding refuge in Spain.

The Peronistas, however, remained politically active and did all they could to disrupt the next governments. For a time there was some stability in the regime of Arturo Frondizi. He worked hard to correct economic problems facing Argentina after decades of mismanagement.

But Frondizi was not as well liked as Perón, who attempted to come back to Argentina in 1964. He was prevented from entering the country and had to return to Spain. Yet even in the next elections, Peronistas showed they could get out the votes. The military was afraid it might not be able to stop Perón. The result was another coup in June, 1966.

Elections for a new government were held in 1973. Guess who showed up? Perón! This time he won, becoming president again. However, Perón became very ill and died on July 1, 1974.

President Isabel Perón confers with her ministers and advisers at the Casa Rosada Government House.

According to the constitution, he was to be succeeded by his vice-president, who was his widow. Perón had married again while in exile. The latest Señora Perón, María Estela (Isabel) Martínez de Perón, took over the Argentine government. She was the first woman to be chief of state of any American nation.

AN ISLAND WAR

Isabel Martínez de Perón was not received as well as Evita. The Argentine political scene fell apart. Kidnapping, killing, and rioting became commonplace. The angry military stepped in and deposed Señora Perón. Another military junta ruled.

After that time, several officers held power: Jorge Videla, Roberto Viola, Leopoldo Galtieri, and Reynaldo Benito Antonio Bignone—all generals.

The latter took office in the summer of 1982. The other generals were upset at Galtieri because he was in power when the Argentines lost the Malvinas Islands war with Great Britain. A return to civilian rule was promised by January, 1984, and elections were held in October, 1983. Raúl Alfonsín, a moderate lawyer and former congressman, was the winner after a hard fought compaign. A member of the Radical party, he gained the presidency in an upset over the Peronist candidate Italo Luder. This was a surprise to the Peronistas because they had won every free election since the party was founded in 1945.

The biggest issues in the campaign were the state of the economy and rearmament after the Malvinas-Falkland war with the British. When the British retook the islands, half the Argentine air force was wiped out. The country's only cruiser, the *General Belgrano,* was sunk. More than one thousand Argentine military died. So after the war, the discredited military grudgingly agreed to the elections.

ECONOMIC DISASTER

The new administration faced a huge foreign debt of about $45 billion. This nightmare started in the 1970s when international bankers lent the country much money, then had to lend more so Argentina could pay the interest on previous loans. The peso was devalued which meant it earned less. By mid-1983 it was worth about 49,000 to the United States dollar.

A revamped monetary system was devised in 1983 in which 10,000 old pesos equaled one new peso. In 1985 the austral replaced the peso. By 1989 with inflation averaging 4,900 percent, President Carlos Saul Menem initiated a currency program converting the austral, renaming it the peso. It was tied to the U.S. dollar at one peso per dollar. Inflation that averaged 9.3 percent by 1992, rose to 40 percent in 1993. Reform measures continue.

Above: A section of the port of Buenos Aires
Below: Cutting alfalfa near San Luis on the western edge of the pampa

Chapter 5

NOT QUITE A ONE-CITY COUNTRY

There has always been an obvious difference between the sprawling city of Buenos Aires and the rest of Argentina. All through the country's history, the Port City has looked outward to Europe and expanded trade. The cities of the interior have been more conservative. They are tied to a rural, traditional way of life.

Today there are still elements of the conflict between the *porteños* of Buenos Aires and the *caudillos* of the pampa.

AN INTERNATIONAL CAPITAL

Buenos Aires attracted residents from numerous nations. This has given the capital an international flavor. It always has seemed to favor the latest in European fashion, art, decor, and food. In contrast, the interior has been more "American," feeling that local customs are often the best.

Economically, this has led to problems. In the past, the

Crowded slums of Buenos Aires

communities of the interior did not look outward for their trade. But Buenos Aires has always been more worldly-minded, wanting to make goods for sale overseas.

All these factors led to political turmoil, bloodshed, and bitterness. However, many of the more obvious problems have slowly been resolved over the past decades. Over the past few years, a flood of immigrants has moved to recently opened agricultural areas in the interior. They took new ideas with them. Previously, many rural people had gone the other way, moving to the cities. Sometimes they would live in *villas de miserias,* or slums. But at least they had been exposed to urban life, for better or worse. Today's "reverse settlers" hope that their skills will help their country and, of course, improve their own economic lot. That was often hard to do in the crowded cities.

But obvious differences remain between urban and rural life-styles. The gaucho mentality, that love of open spaces and freewheeling way of doing things, is very much alive in the farming communities. The people there are very clannish, independent, and often more cautious politically than are citizens in the large towns and cities. For these reasons, some *porteños* still look down their noses at the people from the interior. Unfortunately, this is the case in many Western nations, not just in Argentina.

Buenos Aires remains the most important city in Argentina. In Latin America it is second in size only to Mexico City. The capital spreads over 77 square miles (200 square kilometers). In its center is the Plaza de Mayo. This is the city square near which are most of the important government buildings.

The Casa Rosada is the presidential palace. It is painted pink and is lovely to see when the warm sun washes its walls.

José de San Martín, the famous Argentine general, is buried in the cathedral not far from the Casa Rosada. Down the street, in the Plaza de la Republica, is a tall monument marking the four-hundredth anniversary of the city's founding. It is surrounded by velvety green lawns and cheery gardens, making it a favorite place to meet friends.

The Paseo Colón, one of the major streets, runs to the waterfront. Nearby, Pedro de Mendoza founded the first fort of Buenos Aires so many years ago. The port district is called the Boca. It is a lively Italian neighborhood with taverns, restaurants, and dance halls. The Corrientes is called the "Street That Never Sleeps." It is always packed with people going to film theaters, all-night bookstores, and restaurants.

Buenos Aires is a major world port with freighters from many

Some areas in Buenos Aires that commemorate historical events are the Avenida 9 de Julio (above), that celebrates Independence Day, July 9, 1816, and the Plaza de Mayo (below), which recalls independence from the Spanish viceroys on May 25, 1810.

Above: The Casa Rosada, which houses the offices of Argentina's president, was originally built as a fortress to protect the city. Below: Parks are found throughout Buenos Aires and are ideal for a little relaxation.

The harbor area (left) and an entrance to the subway (right) in Buenos Aires

nations at dockside. Passenger ships leave for exotic locales, including Antarctica. The Río de la Plata is now very polluted, however, due to the water traffic.

Most citizens get around by public transportation. The subway, nicknamed the *subte,* leads to outlying areas and is an inexpensive way to get around.

THEATERS AND MUSEUMS

Buenos Aires is a city of theaters. More than twenty resident companies are very active, staging everything from "underground" drama to the classics. The Teatro Colón is one of

The Teatro Colón is not only home to great opera, but also headquarters for the National Ballet Theater and the National Symphony Orchestra.

the world's greatest opera houses. Many famous performers have sung here. The Colón has a main stage more than a block long, great chandeliers, and banquet halls done in red plush upholstery. The 1989 recession and inflation prolonged renovations to the Colón, but a later 1991 opening showed off a computer-controlled system for moving sets quickly and quietly.

"Theater" of another kind is seen in cattle and sheep markets that still make Buenos Aires the center of South America's auction world. The markets are loud, smelly, and exciting. Animals and processed meats are shipped worldwide from Buenos Aires.

Buenos Aires is a heaven for anyone who enjoys visiting museums. There are at least seventy major buildings with displays from presidential memorabilia to stamps and Teatro Colón theater items.

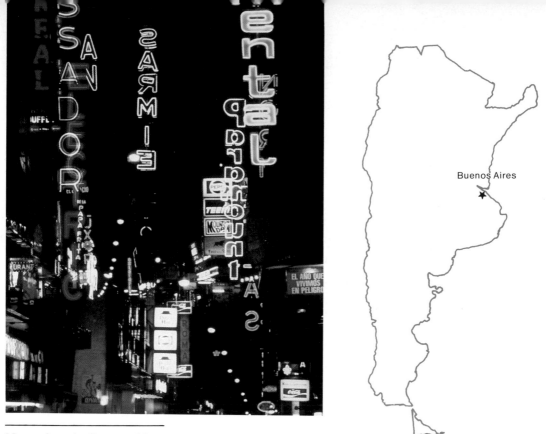

Neon signs in Buenos Aires

Folks in Buenos Aires are avid readers. There are more than eight hundred bookstores in the city. The National Library is another favorite place to browse. The library, with more than 500,000 books and 10,000 manuscripts, dates from 1810.

Anybody visiting Buenos Aires is advised to wear good walking shoes. There are many shops to explore and out-of-the way historical sites, as well as nearly 100 art galleries, 250 film theaters, 500 nightclubs, and 6,000 restaurants.

Few really old buildings remain in the city. Most have been destroyed by fire or warfare over the generations. So Buenos Aires is now a bustling modern city, with towering business buildings. However, ringing the city are slums typical of those surrounding so many of the world's urban areas.

The busiest vacation season in Mar del Plata is from December until Easter.

This is not to say that no one lives in the pampa anymore, just because the capital is crowded. Cities outside Buenos Aires are important as well.

CITIES OF THE COUNTRYSIDE

Some are resort towns, such as Mar del Plata, about four-and-a-half hours by train from the capital. During the November to Easter vacation season more than two million visitors cram into town! They are attracted to the beautiful beaches and the swinging night life. Mar del Plata has a huge gambling casino, with profits going to the welfare ministry.

La Falda, a tourist attraction in Sierra del Córdoba

Córdoba is the capital of Córdoba Province high in the Andes. This very old town, founded in 1573, is Argentina's second-largest city. Córdoba's university was founded in 1613, making it the oldest in the country.

Nearby is a large lake formed by a dam on the Río Primero. Tourists flock here from all over Argentina for fun and rest.

One of the most northern cities of Argentina is San Salvador de Jujuy. The Indians burned it to the ground in 1575, but the Spanish rebuilt in 1593.

Throughout the countryside around Jujuy are many old monasteries and churches. They were built by missionaries in the first days of colonization.

San Salvador de Jujuy, founded in 1593, is the capital of Jujuy, the northernmost province in Argentina.

Mendoza is also in the Andes. From here, San Martín set out with his revolutionary troops to cross the mountains. A terrible earthquake destroyed the city in 1861. Today, most of the rebuilt modern buildings are low, as a precaution against future quakes. On the west side of the city is the Parque San Martín with a huge monument to the general. One section shows Argentine women giving him their jewels. San Martín used the gems to raise money to pay his hungry troops.

Towns in the Chaco are very old. In fact, Santiago del Estero was founded in 1553, making it the oldest of all Argentine cities. Its location on the Río Dulce made it an important trading center. A museum in town displays thousands of pieces of Indian pottery.

Rosario, the third most important city in Argentina, is the capital of Santa Fe Province in Mesopotamia. It is a huge industrial city. Shipments of agricultural items flow through its terminals for overseas sales. It is one of the most bustling of all the interior towns.

PARKS AND PETROCHEMICALS

There are few major cities in Patagonia. The lake district in the north has quite a few resort towns, such as Bariloche with its Swiss style architecture. The town is near the Argentine National Park.

The central feature of this 3,031 square-mile (7,850 square-kilometer) park is Lake Colhué Huapi. The lake covers 205 square miles (531 square kilometers) and is one of the largest in Argentina. Many wild animals and birds live in the forests surrounding the lake. Several excursion boats take visitors to the lake islands.

The only large town in Patagonia is Comodoro Rivadavia. It is the center for Argentina's oil production. A petrochemical plant is the main employer. Until the British-Argentine war of 1982, the town was the jumping-off point for travelers visiting the Malvinas-Falkland Islands. At that time, all air traffic was cut from the mainland to the rocky Atlantic outposts, but is now restored.

Each district and city in Argentina has a distinctive character. All are proud of their local histories. They are eager to keep strong ties to the past. So it is not always a happy occasion when a family decides to move. The new migrants are like the Spanish explorers, whether they move to a city or to the interior. They leave everything behind in a quest for a better life, believing they can find a bright new future wherever they go.

Above: Hotel Llao-Llao, in the Andes, is where Isabel Peron was held under house arrest in 1976. Below: The Gulf of San Jorge in Patagonia

Buenos Aires ★

San Carlos
de Bariloche
●

● Comodoro Rivadavia

*A granite pit in Santa Cruz (above) and
a carpet factory in Catamarca (below)*

Chapter 6

THE ECONOMIC
LOOKING GLASS

When General Reynaldo Bignone was sworn in as president of Argentina in 1982, he asked his fellow citizens for help in restructuring the country's economy. "We will make full use of our potential," he said.

That potential for bigger things has always been a point in Argentina's favor. It is rich in natural resources. It is rich in talented people. Combining the two can only be good for the nation.

Long an agricultural country, Argentina is now taking advantage of its oil and gas reserves. It is increasing its industrial output, especially in chemical manufacturing. There are new factories, dams, and roads.

Argentine gaucho

THE LAND: AN UNBROKEN TRADITION

Yet even in a world of machines and factories, Argentines still carry a love of the earth in their hearts. The Spanish Creole cultures were tied closely to the land. The provincial cities received most of their early wealth from crops and cattle. It's a hard tradition to forget.

This agrarian culture is symbolized by the gaucho, the Argentine cowboy. He was usually poor, living in the open and leading a very rugged life. In the 1700s, the mounted gauchos would speed after herds of cattle. With *boleadoras*, a lasso with balls at one end, they would lash the back legs of stampeding bulls

Implements of the gauchos can be seen in the José Hernández Museum in Buenos Aires. Hernández immortalized the gaucho life in his book Martín Fierro.

or cows. The animals would then crumple to the ground, where they could be killed.

The gaucho was armed only with a knife and the *boleadoras.* He wore a huge poncho that was like a cape. It kept him warm and dry. The gaucho loved singing and dancing. His was a very masculine oriented society, where bravery was considered very important. Today, the gaucho's life seems tamer. It still involves rounding up and branding cattle, but the gaucho now also performs other farm chores. Many gauchos have now moved to cities to look for better paying industrial jobs.

The gaucho's old free and roaming way of life ended when the vast estates were broken up by fences and highways. But the spirit is still there amid the tractors, farm worker unions, and the other trappings of twentieth-century society.

Although most Argentines prefer meat, seafood such as king crab (left) is available. Grapes from the San Rafael vineyard (right) are used to make some fine wine. Argentina is among the top five wine producing countries.

A large portion of the immigrants who flocked to Argentina were skilled farmers, knowledgeable in the ways of the earth. They turned the "desert" into richer, more productive lands. It was through their efforts that Argentina became the granary of the world. Corn, wheat, soybeans, and sorghum are principal crops. Grapes, sugarcane, tobacco, cotton, and tea are also important.

Beef raising is still a major industry. The cattle seem happy grazing on the lush pampa grass. Aberdeen Angus, Shorthorn, Hereford, and Charolais are best for meat production. Holando Argentino cows are fine milk producers. The Argentines use everything but the moo when it comes to processing their animals. Horns, hides, hair, and tongue—everything is valuable. Forty thousand dairies process milk. Argentine cheese is highly praised.

This shorn wool will be processed and exported.

Poultry, hogs, goats, and sheep are also raised all over Argentina. Wool and mutton are world famous for their high quality. Recently, Argentina has produced as much as 153,000 tons (138,000 metric tonnes) of wool annually. That's a lot of yarn for a lot of sweaters.

There are fifty some nations that heavily depend on Argentine farm products. They include large countries such as Russia and smaller countries in Asia and Africa.

With access to the Atlantic Ocean, it is natural for some Argentines to go fishing as a business. About 466,533 tons (420,300 metric tonnes) of fish and seafood are processed annually for internal sale, as well as for export. Many species are netted and brought ashore for processing. A large shellfish from the shrimp family, the langostino, is a very important ocean product. The freshwater pejerrey, a sort of kingfish, is also significant.

Coal mine in Patagonia

NATURAL RESOURCES: MINERALS AND POWER

Argentina is now capitalizing on other natural resources. It has many oil fields. A state operated utility, the Yaciminetos Petroliferos Fiscales (YPF), helped private corporations find new wells. The industry was deregulated in 1991.

These wells have supplied at least 93 percent of the oil needs in Argentina. Thousands of miles of pipeline connect the fields with processing plants.

The country has other mineral riches as well. There is enough natural gas to last at least another one hundred years, according to government reports. Important coal deposits are found in far southern Argentina. More than 560,550 tons (505,000 metric tonnes) are mined annually by Hierro Patagonico, the company that directs the operations.

The spectacular Iguaçu Falls are formed by the union of the Iguaçu and Paraná rivers. This area is preserved as a national park, but other surging rivers are used to create energy.

Power plants are needed to run Argentine industry. Many of the swiftest rivers have been harnessed by dams. The rushing water powers turbines that produce electrical energy. Often, if the river is along a border, Argentina and its neighbor will cooperate in building a power plant. Such a project was recently constructed on the Uruguay River between Argentina and Uruguay. Both countries benefited.

Argentina was the first South American country to have a nuclear power station. It opened in 1974 at Atucha, 62 miles (100 kilometers) north of Buenos Aires. There are now two nuclear power stations in operation. The Atucha facility has also been a training site for technicians from other Latin American countries. Several other plants were being constructed in the 1980s. Six are to be in operation by the year 2000. The country can even mine its own uranium as fuel.

Scientists are studying numerous forms of power production. They have been testing wind, tidal, and solar devices.

Argentina is attempting to be as independent as possible. However, the nation realizes it must live and work with other countries. For that reason, Argentina has been a member of the Association for Latin American Integration. This eleven-member organization signed an economic self-help treaty in 1980. Each country agreed to assist the others in improving conditions at home. It was hoped that everyone would benefit when trade restrictions were relaxed.

Argentina also belonged to the Latin American Economic System (LAES). This organization acted as spokesman for the member countries at international meetings. Argentina is a member of the United Nations (UN), Inter-American Development Bank (IDB), the Organization of American States (OAS), and in 1991 joined Brazil, Uruguay, and Paraguay in signing a Southern Common Market Agreement (MERCOSUR), which is to become effective in 1995.

TRANSPORTATION: OVER AND UNDER

The national merchant marine formerly hauled as much as 50 percent of goods produced in Argentina. This service was important to a country that has always depended on the sea as its contact with the outside world. Argentine shipping was divided into two parts. Ocean travel was handled by the State Merchant Fleet and domestic travel on rivers was under the direction of the Flota Fluvial del Estado Argentina. Most services are now privatized. Shipping is augmented by transportation from the interior to the ports. Roads radiate out from Buenos Aires to the provinces, a heritage from colonial days. The total distance of main roads is

More people and farm products are transported over highways than by rail.

more than 23,194 miles (37,320 kilometers), with more than 111,870 miles (180,000 kilometers) of secondary roads and 487,200 miles (800,000 kilometers) of country roads.

There is one private car for every six Argentines.

Argentina is such a vast country that it needs an extensive, well-kept highway system. There were many challenges to road builders, especially the tall and rugged Andes. Often it is easier to tunnel through the rock than to build over or around peaks.

One example of such engineering is the Christ Redeemer tunnel that links Argentina's main highway, Number 7, with Chile's Highway Number 60. The tunnel is 10,106 feet (3,080 meters) long, with thousands of feet of approach roads. It was opened in May, 1980, amid much fanfare.

The Puerto Unzue-Fray Bentos bridge on the frontier between Argentina and Uruguay is another amazing structure. It is 7,756 feet (2,364 meters) long. Constructing another highway-bridge structure involved moving 390 million cubic feet (11 million cubic meters) of earth. The Argentines enjoy doing things in a big way.

Slabs of beef are stretched out to dry in the sun. Argentina is a leading producer of meat for domestic and foreign markets.

Between 1880 and 1914, Argentina became one of the world's major exporters of produce and meat. It was important to get goods to the ports quickly and inexpensively. British investors saw a chance to make some money. They put a lot of capital behind railroads in Argentina.

By World War I, Argentina had a first-rate system that still links all parts of the country. Annually, the trains carry 10,651 million passengers and millions of tons of cargo over its thousands of miles of track.

As with other countries, the coming of the railroads helped break up the frontier. When the lines were laid across the pampa, settlers followed. The face of Argentina was very different after generations of slow growth.

But some people prefer airplanes. The national airline, *Aerolinas Argentinas,* was 85 percent privatized by 1990. But lack

Aerolinas Argentinas *is the national airline.*

of private funding caused about 33 percent renationalization by 1992. At least ten international and fifty-four other airports make it possible to serve travelers even in frontier areas.

COMMUNICATION: TALKING AND READING

As the country grew closer together, it was necessary to improve the communications systems. Postal and telegraph services, once controlled by the government, are now largely privatized. More than 550 million regular letters and 120 million registered letters have been handled by the electronic processing systems operated by the post office. As many as 40 million telegrams have been sent annually.

The Argentine Post Office has a long tradition. It was founded in 1814. The first telegraph line began operations in 1860, along

The literacy rate in Argentina is over 90 percent.

the tracks of the first Argentine railway.

However, it was not always easy to pick up the phone and call someone in Argentina. Often lines would be jammed as friends talked with each other. The nationalized service, Entel, was privatized in 1990 with now about one telephone per ten persons.

Argentine scientists would like eventually to launch their own communications satellite to handle calls inside Argentina. That might help relieve some of the verbal congestion.

Argentines love reading. There are about 200 daily newspapers published in the country, with the privately owned *Clarin* having the largest circulation in Buenos Aires. Most cities have their own local papers. Even various ethnic groups publish national papers or magazines. The *Southern Cross* is Irish, *Le Quotidien* is French, and *Argentinisches Tageblatt* is German.

The Argentine constitution protects freedom of the press, but usually this was only in the provinces. This freedom did not extend to the Federal District of Buenos Aires, where most of the

La Prensa *newspaper, which was published in this building, was silenced by President Juan Perón for criticizing his policies.*

country's important papers were published. The press was required to constantly be careful not to offend authorities. Under Perón, newspapers would be shut down if they printed editorial opposition to the president's actions. The press learned that self-censorship allowed them to remain in business. In 1993 Menem proposed and the senate unanimously approved repealing the law that had been used to stifle press and public criticism.

There are now numerous state-owned, provincial, municipal, and private radio and television stations that produce programs from news to entertainment. Favorite programs are soccer matches broadcast much like football games in the United States.

The Argentine can look at all this activity, take a deep breath, and wonder where it all will lead. Everyone hopes the economic crisis will continue to improve, so people won't have to worry about inflation and possible devaluation of their money. It will be a long struggle but Argentines are optimistic. They have too much going for them to be discouraged.

An Indian child from the north and a gaucho

Chapter 7

PEOPLE OF THE WORLD

Argentina has always had a very diverse population. Many nationalities have made new homes in this wide and open country. The early settlers were basically *mestizo,* whose fathers were Spaniards and mothers were Indians. However, there were many Creoles, with both parents of Spanish descent. The *mestizos* came from Asunción, Paraguay. The pioneers fled there and built that city after Indians destroyed Buenos Aires. The Creoles were from the Chilean and Peruvian sides of the Andes.

Another major influence on the colonial population was that of blacks and mulattoes. The latter were people whose fathers or mothers were black, white, Indian, or any racial combination. The blacks and mulattoes formed a major portion of the revolutionary armies that battled the Spaniards. They were very brave fighters, but many did not return from the various campaigns. They stayed in Chile, Peru, or Bolivia, which helped to decrease their bloodlines in Argentina. Slavery was abolished in 1813 in Argentina.

MIGRANTS AND IMMIGRANTS

In the nineteenth century, hundreds of thousands of newcomers poured into Argentina. Some were temporary workers from Europe. They were nicknamed "The Swallows" because they came and went across the Atlantic in the spring and fall—at planting and harvest times. Because the seasons were just the opposite of those in their homelands, they could then work on farms all year-round.

In addition to migratory laborers, millions of others arrived. However, because of the social and economic system of the day, most of the newcomers became tenant farmers or workers. Much of the rural countryside was tied up in huge estates. It was hard for a poor immigrant to purchase property.

So most settled in the cities. They worked in the textile mills, the packinghouses, granaries, and flour mills. Many immigrants opened small shops. Entire neighborhoods in Buenos Aires and the other larger towns were totally Italian, German, Irish, Polish, or Jewish. They had their own social clubs, newspapers, and sports. They made Argentina's urban society a rich collection of many traditions. The British who came were skilled office workers, administrators, and professionals. They helped shape the country's industry and commerce.

Some of the immigrants, however, preferred to live in the interior. Many Welsh came to Argentina to herd sheep. There are still some tiny communities where the Welsh language continues to be spoken.

The constitution of 1853 gave all citizens equal rights, regardless of where they were born. Newcomers were welcomed in Argentina. Recently, refugees from war-torn Southeast Asia

A tea shop advertises Welsh tea and a Danish man walks through a flower market. Regardless of their origin, all citizens have equal rights.

found safety in Argentina. They, too, became citizens as well. Such a liberal immigration policy has always been important to Argentina. Juan Bautista Alberdi, a political philosopher and "father of the Argentine constitution," believed that to govern is to populate. He wanted many people to live in his country, not caring about their ancestral backgrounds and ethnic roots. Since the mid-nineteenth century, Argentina was second only to the United States in the Western Hemisphere in welcoming new citizens.

Children of all these immigrants moved into highly skilled jobs in business, industry, education, science, and literary fields.

*Pope John Paul II meets with President Galtieri in the
Casa Rosada during the pope's 1982 visit to South America.*

A CATHOLIC COUNTRY

Because most of the early immigrants were Roman Catholic,
they were readily accepted into early Argentine society. The first
settlers had been Catholics. The church was very important in
colonial administration. The 1853 constitution made Catholicism
the state religion. The presidents still have to be Catholic. In the
1880s, however, there was a brief surge of anticlericalism, a
movement against all established churches. But that problem
fizzled out after only a few years.

Today, about 90 percent of Argentina's people call themselves
Catholic, although the church is not as strong as it is in some
other South American countries. Most folks are quite casual about
church attendance. However, millions turned out to see and hear
Pope John Paul II say mass when he made a pilgrimage to
Argentina in 1982.

A college student doing her assignments

About 3 percent of the population are Protestants and 2 percent are Jewish.

Women are granted equal rights in Argentina. They often make up 50 percent of the population. Since the 1940s, they have been a major part of the work force. There are women lawyers, doctors, and other professionals. Politically, they are quite active. Witness the governmental roles of President Juan Perón's wives, Eva and Isabel.

Argentina has a strong social security system. There is a pension requirement in business that ensures that people receive money after they retire. There are subsidies for older citizens who were unable to contribute to pension funds. Social welfare funds are also issued according to need. In Argentina, the government takes care of disability payments as well, assisting injured workers who can't return to their jobs.

Sickness, hospitalization, and vacation allowances are worked out between industry and the strong unions. The living standards in Argentina are similar to those of Europe.

Elementary students enjoying a break

EDUCATION

Argentine young people are like youth all around the world. They enjoy music, dancing, going out with friends, playing sports, traveling, and watching films. Almost all youngsters can read or write, even in the remote regions of the country. Education has long been an important responsibility accepted by the government. President Domingo Faustino Sarmiento, who ruled Argentina from 1868 to 1874, was a leader in promoting high standards of education.

Every child has to attend primary school, which is free in state-run schools. Today, there are more than four million youngsters between the ages of six and fourteen attending classes. There are seven years of primary grades. Schools are run by the provinces. The city of Buenos Aires is responsible for its own school

Mathematics class

administration. There are also private schools throughout the country where tuition is charged.

In many schools, the boys and girls wear uniforms. They study many of the same subjects as pupils in other parts of the world: reading, math, science, history, and art.

High school is also free at state schools. There are two divisions: basic and higher. In the basic, pupils learn the fundamentals of harder subjects. In their last two years, they can specialize in several areas, even farming and the arts.

About 500,000 young people attend universities and technical schools. Many adults attend night school. There are many specialty schools—for teachers, for sports instructors, in the arts, and other fields. Argentina can boast of at least twenty-nine national, one provincial, and twenty-three private universities.

Many students go on for higher degrees after they are graduated from a university.

Over the years, the education system has been fairly liberal and well respected. However, during the Perón years, schoolchildren were continually told about the president and his wife, Eva. This very heavy propaganda continued after Señora Perón died. One textbook had a story about her being a star in the sky taking care of Argentina. After Perón died and his third wife was removed from office, this type of material was toned down.

THE SUCCESS OF SCHOLARS

There is a strong love of learning in Argentina. Researchers and scholars are well respected. One important scientist was Florentino Ameghino (1854-1911). He was a world famous anthropologist who studied ancient cultures. Juan Bautista Ambrosetti (1865-1917) loved folk music. He wrote many papers about Indian and colonial music.

Louis Agote (1868-1954) was a medical professor who worked in Buenos Aires's Rawson Hospital. He discovered the first practical method to transfuse blood without it coagulating.

Another Argentine, Juan Vucetich, who lived in the late nineteenth century, is credited with inventing fingerprinting.

Two Argentine scientists have won Nobel Prizes for their work. Bernardo Houssay won the physiology award in 1947 and Luis Federico Leloir received the chemistry prize in 1970.

Many Argentines have achieved international recognition for medical studies. Dr. Rene Favaloro and Dr. Domingo Liotta are known for heart research.

However, in the 1960s, especially during the regime of President Juan Carlos Onganía, many researchers and educators fled Argentina. They did not like the political oppression and the

The University of Cordóba was established in 1613.

instability of the country. Onganía sent troops to take over the University of Buenos Aires in 1966 because the students and faculty were among his most vocal political opponents. There was much fighting and many people died. More than one thousand faculty members left the university in the wake of the turmoil.

Today, that unhappy situation has slowly been resolved. There are more organizations in Argentina that help researchers. They provide money for experiments. Sometimes they provide space in which to work.

Among these groups have been the National Scientific Research Council, the National Farming and National Industrial Technology institutes, the National Institute of Hydraulic Science and Technology, the National Atomic Energy Commission, and many others. Even the military has had research facilities.

Argentina works closely with other nations. It has signed treaties for technical cooperation with at least thirty different countries. It helps the United Nations work with poorer countries.

For their activities in promoting the good of mankind, two Argentines have won the Nobel Peace Prize. This is one of the highest honors anyone can receive. In 1936, Carlos Saavedra Lamas won the coveted honor. At that time, he was Argentine minister of foreign affairs and worship. He worked tirelessly as a mediator to end a war that had erupted between Bolivia and Paraguay. In 1980, Adolfo Pérez Esquivel won the Nobel Peace Prize for helping political prisioners and seeking justice and peace in South America. He has been an outspoken critic of his government's strict policies in silencing political opponents.

His leadership inspired quiet protest on the part of many Argentines whose relatives had been imprisoned or executed because of their politics. There were marches by mothers of the "disappeared ones," those who vanished after being arrested. More than six thousand persons, most of them probably innocent, were seized by government agents as violence increased in the mid-1970s. More than one hundred children under the age of twelve also simply disappeared after being taken into custody. In 1983, the military government finally admitted that most probably died in jail.

HUMAN RIGHTS AND A DIRTY WAR

When Argentina was censured around the world for its position on human rights, the government claimed it acted properly. It felt that critics in other countries didn't understand the problems in Argentina.

Mothers of the "disappeared ones" march every Thursday regardless of weather.

A large book called *The Right To Freedom* explained the government's position. The nation's military leaders felt that strict controls were necessary to prevent terrorism.

They pointed out that former President Pedro Eugenio Aramburu was kidnapped in 1973 and eventually killed by revolutionaries. Many policemen, government officials, and soldiers also had been assassinated. For these reasons, they felt that a firm hand was necessary to prevent anarchy in Argentina.

The junta that replaced Isabel Perón launched a "dirty war" against opponents of the regime. However, after the civilian Raúl Alfonsín was elected, his government began investigating the human-rights tragedy. Many military and law enforcement personnel involved in the antiterrorist campaign were jailed because of their excesses.

Leopoldo Galtieri, the Argentine president who led the country into war with Great Britain over the Malvinas-Falklands, was also arrested, along with some of his major military supporters. Galtieri subsequently was charged with incompetence and negligence in the conduct of the war. The Argentine people hoped that investigations would provide answers to their many questions about disappearances during the 1970s and early 1980s.

WRITERS AND READERS

In spite of restrictions, Argentine writers have always been in the forefront of the South American literary world. Sometimes this world spills over into politics.

President Sarmiento wrote a classic story about a *caudillo* and his family. The book, entitled *Facundo*, is considered a masterpiece.

José Hernández, who was also active in national politics, wrote *Martín Fierro*. This was a long poem about the gauchos. In the 1920s, a group of young writers called themselves the "Martinfierristas," after Hernández's hero.

A well-known member of this informal club was Jorge Luis Borges. He was nominated several times for the Nobel Prize in literature. By the mid-1980s, Borges had become a crusty conservative, but still was a literary lion considered to be South America's greatest poet.

The list of Argentine authors could go on almost forever. There's Eduardo Mallea, Ricardo Guiraldes, Ezequiel Martinez Estrada, Conrade Nale Roxlo, Macedonio Fernandez, and dozens of others.

Victoria Ocampo spent a fortune publishing a magazine called *Sur*. Its pages were filled with magnificent stories and poems by

Jorge Luis Borges, poet, essayist, and short-story writer

Argentine authors. She also supported the work of writers from around the world. For years, *Sur* was considered one of the best literary magazines anywhere. Authors were very proud to be published by Señora Ocampo.

The country boasts of at least eight thousand bookstores. Many are open twenty-four hours a day. A major book fair is held every year in Buenos Aires. A recent exhibition attracted 700,000 visitors.

Argentina publishes thousands of books a year. Of course, many have small circulations, averaging five thousand or so. But the figures are still remarkable. There have been as many as two hundred publishing houses producing ten or more books a year.

Intellectuals are among the most prominent figures in South America. Argentina is no exception. Because of their education and ability to say what is on their minds, the country's intellectuals are admired by both the rich and the poor. Sometimes this got them into trouble with the government, but they carried on. By the 1990s this censorship changed.

Above: La Boca, the old port area of Buenos Aires where the tango
originated, has gaily painted restaurants, homes, and art galleries.
Below: Many of Argentina's folk dances originated with the gauchos.

Chapter 8

LAND OF THE TANGO

Many countries have national dances. Chile has the *quecha*. Ireland has the jig. Scotland has the Highland fling. The United States has the square dance.

And Argentina has the tango.

The tango evolved from many musical forms, basically from the polka and a Spanish dance called the *habanera*. The music of black freedmen who lived in the Río de la Plata area was an influence. By the end of the nineteenth century, today's classical tango was recognizable.

At first it was music of the gauchos and the lower classes of workers. But Europeans fell in love with it in the 1920s. Upper-class Argentines then began dancing the tango as well. The *bandoneon,* a cross between an accordion and a concertina, is the primary instrument in tango music. Violins and other instruments can be included as well. The *bandoneon* was brought to Argentina by German sailors.

La Boca remembers the tango and the king of the tango, Carlos Gardel.

There have been many classical tango composers, including Francisco Canaro, who introduced the tango to Japan! Astor Piazolla is an internationally famous *bandoneon* player who has written scores for films. He also composed a ballet score for Moscow's Bolshoi Theater. A famous tango singer, Carlos Gardel, died years ago, but his records still sell well. Tango fans say that ''Gardel sings better every day.'' They mean that nobody has ever been as good as Gardel.

MUSIC AND DANCE

Argentines love music. The first missionaries stressed the importance of learning music and taught classes in their frontier schools. Many Argentines have become great composers. Amancio Alcorta (1805-1862) is considered the first native Argentine composer. The operas of Arturo Beruti (1862-1938) are known around the world.

Teatro Colón

Next to the tango, opera must be the most popular music in Argentina. Fifty Argentine operas have debuted in their home country and eighteen others were first produced abroad. As early as 1825, operas were staged in Buenos Aires. It's not uncommon to hear street musicians singing beautiful arias.

More popular musical compositions have been written by Felipe Boero, Pascual de Rogatis, Alberto Williams, Carlos Guastavino, and Alberto Ginastera. Noted orchestra leaders have been Mariano Drago and Juan José Castro.

Ballet seems to have captured the fancy of Argentines, just as did the tango. The names of *Argentinita*, Liliana Belfiore, Olga Ferri, Norma Fontenla, José Neglia, and Iris Scaccheri recall images of their grace and composure on the stage. Choreographer Oscar Araiz is said to have directed some of the best dances ever presented in South America.

Besides works by Argentine playwrights, theaters also present translations of foreign plays, stand-up comics, and revues.

THEATER AND FINE ARTS

Argentine playwrights have been hard at work since colonial days. *Siripo,* written by Manuel de Lavarden in the late 1700s, is thought to be among the first plays written by a native Argentine. Enrique Garcia Velloso wrote a massive play in 1901, entitled *Jesus Nazareno.* He packed theaters in South America and Europe with his subsequent creations. Roberto Payro is known for his social commentary. His plays criticized the old-time Creoles and their life-styles.

There are at least 270 theaters in Argentina, not counting halls belonging to social and sport clubs where plays can be presented. Argentine actors and actresses Elsa O'Connor, Mecha Ortiz, Lea Conti, Osvaldo Terranova, Sergio Renan, Pepe Soriano, and

Creations by local artists

Alfredo Alcon have been among the most popular stage performers.

The visual arts in Argentina, painting and sculpture, only recently have been recognized for their quality. In colonial times, most of the art dealt with religious themes. Many of the church decorations were imported. It wasn't until the 1830s, when Carlos Morel and Fernando García Molina began exhibiting, that native Argentine artists became well known.

In 1896, the National Museum of Fine Arts was opened. This gave a big boost to Argentine art. Finally there was a central place, of national stature, in which to exhibit works. Soon, the names of Argentines became world famous. Quinquela Martin painted scenes from the docks in Buenos Aires. Pedro Figari enjoyed painting about old-time city life.

Fans crowd La Bonbonera Stadium to watch a soccer game.

Sculptors such as Lucio Fontana and Fernando Arranz are among the many artists who work in marble, ceramics, clay, and similar substances.

Today, there are more than one hundred art galleries in Buenos Aires. Each year, at least six thousand shows are held. And that doesn't include the many galleries that present exhibitions in the provincial cities.

Then there's sports.

WORLD CUPS AND LIVE DUCKS

There are few other countries that love "futbol" (football or soccer) as does Argentina. The British brought the sport to South America in the nineteenth century. Soon everyone was playing.

Argentine teams are noted for their finesse in handling the ball. They are very emotional, but skilled, players who attack and defend with equal ease. The top players are always featured in newspapers and sporting magazines.

The Argentines captured the World Cup championship in 1978 in front of a happy home-country crowd in Buenos Aires, rolling over the most powerful soccer nations of the world.

The stands went crazy when team captain Daniel Pasarella ran around the field with the huge trophy after the final game. He and his teammates were national heroes.

In 1979, an Argentine youth team won the Junior World Championship played in Japan.

At the height of the 1982 Malvinas-Falklands war with the British, both England and Argentina competed in the World Cup games in Madrid, Spain. Hundreds of millions of people all over the world watched on television. But the two teams never met on the field because both were edged out in the quarter finals. Argentina lost the war over control of the Falklands, but it did better on the soccer field a few years later. In 1986 it recaptured the World Cup at the games held in Mexico, defeating West Germany in the final game.

Professional auto racing seems to come naturally for some Argentines. Since the 1950s, they have burned up the tracks in a dozen countries. Juan Manuel Fangio was world champion driver five times. Carlos Alberto Reutemann has been a top notch Grand Prix driver. Ricardo Zunino is one of the younger, more formidable drivers of recent years.

Horsepower of another sort is evidenced in the rough and tumble game of *pato*, which originated with the gauchos. In the

The ball used in pato *has handles so the players can pass it from one to another.*

old days, a live duck (*pato* in Spanish) was stuffed into a sack. Only its head would stick out. Two teams of horsemen fought over the sack, racing back and forth over a three-mile-long (five-kilometer) field.

The game often degenerated into a bloody brawl and was banned in 1822. However, it soon reappeared under the administration of President Juan Manuel de Rosas, who was a fan of anything connected with the gaucho culture. The Argentine Pato Federation was founded in 1941, with forty clubs. It is not quite so violent now because a large ball is used instead of a frightened duck. The game is similar to polo, which is also popular in Argentina — thanks to the British. The players in *pato*, however, grab the ball with their hands instead of hitting it with a mallet as in polo. They then try to stuff the ball into a large net, in order to score points.

A statue of boxer Luis Angel Firpo has been placed outside his mausoleum.

Since the 1940s, Argentine polo teams have won many gold medals in Olympic games, as well as numerous other awards for their spirited play. The gaucho and Araucanian tradition of fine horsemanship is still evident.

Argentine boxers are well known in the sports world. A major fighter in the 1920s, was Luis Angel Firpo. He was nicknamed "The Wild Bull of the Pampas." His best-known fight was in 1923, when he knocked world heavyweight champion Jack Dempsey out of the ring. Dempsey, of the United States, came back to win the match.

Unfortunately, Firpo was never able to gain the heavyweight crown, but eight other Argentines have been world champions in various weight classes since his day. Carlos Monzón was middleweight champ from 1970 to 1977. He was not defeated in fourteen challenges to his crown.

A popular form of relaxation is sitting at a sidewalk café.

There are many other sports heroes in Argentina. The country's ice hockey team was world champion in 1978. Many records in swimming have been set by Argentines. Golfer Roberto De Vicenzo, marathon runners Juan Carlos Zabala and Delfo Cabrera, and tennis players Guillermo Vilas, José Luis Clerc, and Ivanna Madruga are highly respected.

Argentina is a café society. Townspeople enjoy sitting at a sidewalk table, sipping sodas or coffee and watching the passersby. A favorite café game is chess. From the cafés, Argentine chess players have moved out to challenge the best players of other countries. Many of the better players are young people. Oscar Panno was world champion juvenile in 1952. Carlos Bielicki was world champion juvenile in 1957. Marcelo Tempone was world cadet champion in 1979.

PARADES AND HOLIDAYS

The Argentines seem tireless in their sports and their pursuit of culture. When they finally do slow down, it's time for a meal, a party, or a festival. Argentina has several national holidays, which are always good for parades and speeches. January 1 is New Year's Day. A huge parade takes place through downtown Buenos Aires each New Year's Eve. Cars and buses are decorated with long rolls of colored paper and streamers.

Good Friday is a somber holiday, just before the happy feast of Easter. Everyone goes to church on those two religious observances. May 1 is Labor Day. All the unions turn out for parades and parties.

May 25 is the anniversary of the Revolution of 1810, followed by June 20, Flag Day. Independence Day is July 9, with August 17 being the anniversary of the death of General San Martín. December 25, is of course, Christmas Day and the chance to exchange presents.

Other public holidays include Maundy Thursday, just before Easter, and December 8, the Catholic feast of the Immaculate Conception. Banks and public offices are closed on those days, but businesses can remain open. Each provincial city also celebrates the anniversary of its founding.

FROM BEEF TO PIZZA

Central to the holidays is a big meal. Since Argentina is such a major beef producer, the country's national dishes use a lot of meat. The *asado* is a roast cooked over an open fire. *Bif a caballo* is a steak topped with an egg. *Carbonada* is made with minced beef,

Cooks dressed as gauchos roast beef, veal, and lamb over an open pit (above).
A favorite fruit of the Argentines is tuna (below), the fruit of the prickly pear cactus.

Lago Mascardi in the Bariloche area

onions, and tomatoes. *Empanada* is a meat pie, something like a meat pasty. *Noquis* are potato dumplings served with meat and a tomato sauce. They are inexpensive and favorite restaurant items for children.

Everyone who visits Argentina should sample *locro*. This is a heavy soup made with corn, white beans, pumpkin, beef, and lots of other items. It is sort of a catchall, and delicious.

The Italian influence is seen with the range of pasta dishes. Pizza can be purchased just about anywhere. Italian style ice cream is also popular.

Dulce de leche is a dessert guaranteed to tickle a sweet tooth. It is made of milk and sugar, beaten into a sort of fudge. Argentines eat cheese with *dulce de leche* to cut down on the sweet taste.

Argentina is certainly an exciting country, full of grand surprises and great traditions. It would be fun to be a gaucho for a time. Or to sit at a sidewalk café. Or to get a suntan at Mar del Plata. All that is possible in Argentina, a world of enchantment.

MAP KEY

Cerro Aconcagua (peak)	G3	Cerro Ojos del Salado	F4
Azul	G5	Pampa de las Salinas	G4
Bahía Blanca	G4	Paraná	G5
Bermejo River	F5	Paraná River	G5
Bolívar	G4	Pilcomayo River	F4
Buenos Aires	G5	Río de la Plata	G5
Catamarca	F4	Posadas	F5
Chico River	H4	Pta. Rasa (point)	H4
Chubut River	H4	Rawson	H4
Colorado River	G4	Resistencia	F5
Comodoro Rivadavia	H4	Río Cuarto	G4
Córdoba	G4	Río Gallegos	I4
Corrientes	F5	Rosario	G4
Deán Funes	G4	Salado River	F4, G4
C. Desengaño (cape)	H4	Salinas Grandes	F4
C. Dos Bahías (cape)	H4	Salta	F4
Esquel	H3	C. San Antonio (cape)	G5
Falkland Islands		San Carlos de Bariloche	H3
(Islas Malvinas)	I4, I5	Gulfo San Jorge (gulf)	H4
Monte Fitz Roy (mountain)	H3	San Juan	G4
Formosa	F5	San Julián	H4
General Acha	G4	San Luis	G4
Goya	F5	Gulfo San Matías (gulf)	H4
Grande de Tierra de Fuego	I4	San Miguel de Tucumán	F4
Volcán Lanín (volcano)	G3	San Salvador de Jujuy	F4
La Plata	G5	Santa Fe	G4
La Rioja	F4	Santa Rosa	G4
Limay River	G4	Santiago del Estero	F4
Strait of Magellan	I4	South Georgia, Falkland Islands	I4
Islas Malvinas		Stanley	I5
(Falkland Islands)	I4, I5	Tandil	G5
Mar del Plata	G5	Tierra del Fuego, Grande de	I4
Mendoza	G4	Trelew	H4
Mercedes	F5	Tres Arroyos	G4
Mercedes	G4	C. Tres Puntas (cape)	H4
Pta. Mogotes (point)	G5	Uruguay River	F5, G5
Negro River	G4	Ushuaia	I4
Neuquén	G4	Península Valdés	H4
Neuquén River	G4	Viedma	H4
		C. Vírgenes (cape)	I4

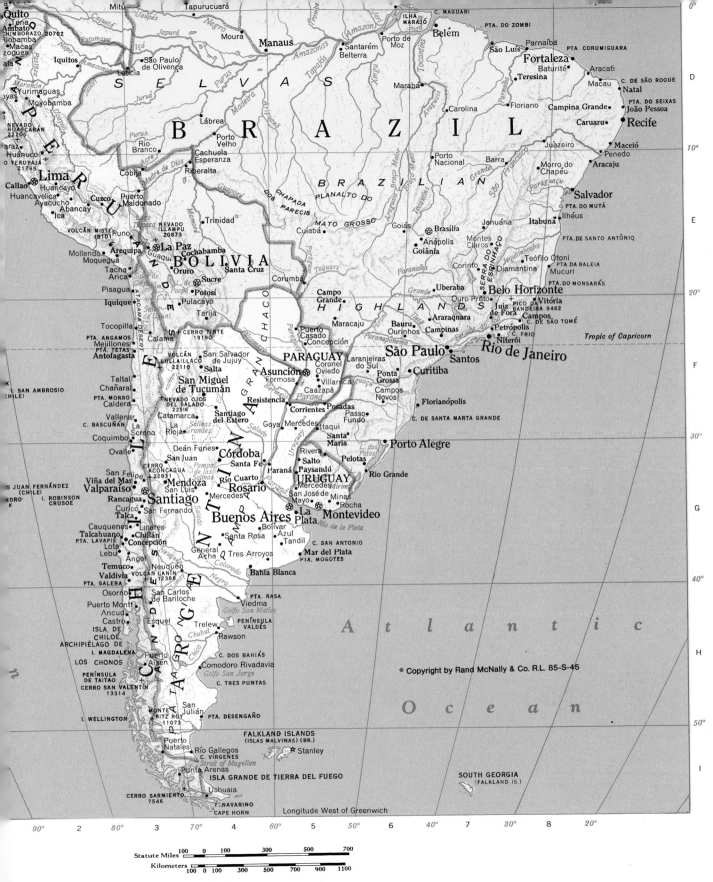

MINI-FACTS AT A GLANCE

GENERAL INFORMATION

Official Name: Argentine Republic (República Argentina)

Capital: Buenos Aires

Official Language: Spanish

Government: Argentina is a republic. The president, who is head of the government, is elected for a six-year term. The Chamber of Deputies, which has 257 members, is like the United States House of Representatives. Members of the Senate, which has 46 members, are nominated by provincial legislatures. There are 23 provinces in Argentina and a Federal District, which includes Buenos Aires. Offshore islands are considered a national territory. All of the provinces have their own governors and legislatures.

Argentina was under the control of military governments from 1976 until December, 1983. During this time, three-member juntas ran the government. They were composed of the chiefs of staff of the army, navy, and air force. They appointed the president, who in turn appointed the cabinet members. Provincial governors were appointed by a president with the junta's approval. During this period, many civil rights were suspended and abuses of power were numerous.

Flag: The national flag is made up of three stripes of equal width: two blue horizontal stripes on either side of a white stripe. In the middle of the white stripe is a sun that represents Argentina's freedom from Spain.

Coat of Arms: The coat of arms features two hands clasped. They are surrounded by a laurel wreath. In the background is a red "liberty cap" mounted on a pole. Atop the laurel wreath is a rising sun. The light blue and white fields in the coat of arms match the colors in the flag.

National Anthem: Words to the national song, *"Himno Nacional Argentino,"* were written in 1812 by Vincente Lopez y Planes. Music is by Blas Parera.

Money: Money in Argentina is measured in pesos, which replaced the austral in January of 1992. Approximately one peso equals one United States dollar.

Weights and Measures: Argentina uses the metric system.

Population: 28,226,920 (1980 estimate); 33,767,000 (1994 estimate)

Cities:

	1980 Census	1990 Estimate
Buenos Aires	2,908,001	2,922,829
Córdoba	968,664	993,055
Rosario	875,623	938,120
La Plata	454,884	477,175
Santa Fe	287,240	292,165
Paraná	159,581	161,638
Mendoza	118,427	101,579

GEOGRAPHY

Highest Point: Mount Aconcagua, 23,831 ft. (6,959 m)

Lowest Point: Valdés Península, 131 ft. (40 m) below sea level

Rivers: Río de la Plata is the largest river in Argentina; it drains an area of 1,600,000 sq. mi. (4,133,981 km²) and has many tributaries. The Río Colorado, the next largest, is 744 mi. long (1,197 km).

Mountains: The vast chain of the Andes forms the western border. The Piedmont, a region of low mountains and desert valleys, is east of the Andes.

Climate: Argentina's seasons are opposite to the seasons in the Northern Hemisphere. Summer runs from December through February and winter from June through August. In January, temperatures average about 80° F. (27° C) in the north and about 50° F. (10° C) in the far south. In July, average temperatures range from 60° F. (16° C) in the north to 32° F. (0° C) in the south.
Rainfall varies in Argentina. There is more in the northeastern part of the country than in the west and south. In Mesopotamia there may be as much as 60 in. (150 cm) a year; in the Piedmont and most of Patagonia, there is usually less than 10 in. (26 cm).

Greatest Distances: North to south—2,300 mi. (3,700 km)
East to west—980 mi. (1,577 km)

Area: 1,073,400 sq. mi. (2,780,092 km²)

NATURE

Trees: Common trees in Argentina include the fir and pine, with apple and other fruit trees cultivated in orchards. Rain forests are thick along the northern borders, with heavy jungle foliage. The *quebracho* tree was once plentiful in the Chaco region, but most of those forests have been cut down. The *quebracho* has very hard wood and is used for fence posts, telephone and telegraph poles, and railroad ties.

Fish: Many species of deep water fish are caught offshore. Herring and salmon are plentiful. Inland waters teem with pike, bass, and other freshwater game fish.

Animals: In the rain forests are jaguars, wild hogs, monkeys, lizards, and many other creatures. Parrots, hummingbirds, and toucans live in the trees. In Patagonia are guanacos (distant relatives to the camel), foxes, armadillos, opossums, cuis (similar to ground squirrels), penguins, rheas (similar to ostriches), red-backed hawks, and many other species. Mountain sheep are sometimes found in the Andes, as are South American condors—among the largest birds in the world.

EVERYDAY LIFE

Food: The Argentines have many cultures that have contributed ethnic dishes. The Italians contributed pizza and many pasta dishes. The English offered meat pies. Many dishes center on beef. *Asado* is beef roasted over an open fire. *Bif a caballo* is a steak crowned with a fried egg. *Noquis* are potato dumplings with a meat and tomato sauce. *Dulce de leche* is a favorite sweet dessert made from milk and sugar. *Almendrado* is ice cream rolled in crushed almonds. Argentine wines are very good. Dairy products are widely available.

Housing: There was a housing shortage in the cities in the 1960s because of the great number of people from rural areas who moved in looking for work. Large shantytowns known as *villas de miserias,* with dwellings made of corrugated iron, became common around big cities. Many of these communities have disappeared as the housing shortage has improved.

Holidays:

> January 1, New Year's Day
> April 2, Invasion of the Malvinas
> Good Friday
> May 1, Labor Day
> May 25, Anniversary of the 1810 Revolution
> June 20, Flag Day
> July 9, Independence Day
> August 17, Death of General José de San Martín
> December 8, Immaculate Conception
> December 25, Christmas

114

Culture: The gaucho, or Argentine cowboy, has been an important influence on many of Argentina's greatest writers. *Martín Fierro*, an epic poem written by José Hernández in the nineteenth century about a gaucho who rebels against society, and Domingo F. Sarmiento's *Civilization and Barbarism: Life of Juan Facundo Quiroga*, written in the middle of the nineteenth century, which takes a less romantic view of the gaucho, are famous examples of works of this kind.

Gauchos have also figured in Argentine art. The most famous Argentine painter, Prilidiano Pueyrredón, painted gauchos and their surroundings in the nineteenth century.

In the twentieth century, a number of Argentine artists have become internationally known, including Jorge Luis Borges, an essayist, poet, and short-story writer; Ernesto Sábato and Julio Cortázar, both novelists; sculptors Julio le Parc and Alicia Penalba; Alberto Ginastera, a composer; and Antonia Mercé, an Argentine ballerina who was the leading dancer with the Madrid Opera from 1899 to 1902 and popularized the neoclassical style of Spanish dance. She was known as *Argentinita*.

Sports and Recreation: Argentines' favorite game is "futbol" (soccer). Argentina won a world championship in 1978 and its athletes have played well in many international tournaments. Tennis, rugby, chess, skiing, auto racing, boxing, ice hockey, and boat racing are also popular, as is polo, which was introduced by the English. Rodeos with roping and riding contests attract enthusiastic crowds. At the most important rodeo, each May at Ayacucho, Argentines from all over the country participate.

Communication: There are about 125 radio stations in Argentina. They are owned by the state, provincial governments, city governments, and universities, and others are privately owned. The principal stations are in Buenos Aires. In 1991, there were about 21,582,000 radio receivers. There are four television channels in Buenos Aires alone. About 8,000,000 television sets are in use in Argentina.

There are about two hundred daily newspapers in Argentina and hundreds of periodicals of all kinds. The Argentine constitution protects freedom of the press in the provinces but not in the Federal District, which contains Buenos Aires and most of the country's important newspapers. Freedom of the press has always been fragile, even when the constitution was in effect. Journalists have been arrested for publishing material that challenged the government. Some publications were banned by the government. By the 1990s censorship laws were repealed.

Transportation: Only about 25 percent of Argentina's roads are paved. Yet, they carry more of the passenger traffic and goods to market than do railroads. There are about 136,017 mi. (220,093 km) of main and secondary roads and 25,000 mi. (40,000 km) of railroad track. Air travel has become very important to offset the limitations of ground travel. There are over two hundred airports. Major seaports are Buenos Aires, La Plata, Rosario, and Bahía Blanca.

Schools: Education is considered very important in Argentina. The country has one of the highest literacy rates in the world. Education is free from preschool to the university level. It is compulsory for children ages six to fourteen. There are several different kinds of secondary education programs that last from four to six years. There are twenty-nine state universities and twenty-three private universities. There is also higher education that is not taught in the university. Teachers go to school for three or four years to become qualified in a nonuniversity setting.

Health and Social Welfare: Argentina is a very health-conscious nation with one doctor for every 370 people as of the late 1980s. A strong social security system protects retired and disabled workers. Most retired workers receive pensions. Those who don't are assisted by the government. Contributions to the system are provided by the workers on the job. Trade unions and private social agencies also offer insurance and benefit plans.

Principal Products:
Agriculture: Beef, frozen and canned fish, dairy products, wheat, corn, soybeans, sunflower seeds, flaxseed, grapes, citrus fruits, sugar, tobacco
Manufacturing: Automobiles, steel, heavy machinery, textiles, processed foods
Power resources: Coal, gas, and oil

IMPORTANT DATES

1516—Juan Díaz de Solís sails up Río de la Plata and is killed by Indians

1520—Magellan lands on Patagonia

1536—Pedro de Mendoza builds a fort called Buenos Aires

1541—Buenos Aires burned by Indians

1553—Spanish settlers from Peru establish Santiago del Estero, the first permanent town in Argentina

1561-1562—Spanish settlers from Chile establish Mendoza and San Juan

1580—Buenos Aires rebuilt by expedition from Asunción

1592—Malvinas Islands discovered by English explorer John Davis

1617—Buenos Aires district given its own governor

1766-1777—Disputes with England over Malvinas-Falkland Islands

1776—Viceroyalty of the Río de la Plata established with seat of power in Buenos Aires

1778—Trade permitted between Argentina and Europe

1806—English occupy Buenos Aires but Argentines under Santiago Liniers force them to surrender; Liniers made viceroy

1807—British again attack Buenos Aires but are defeated

1810—Argentine junta rejects Spanish authority; the Buenos Aires cabildo (town council) declares independence

1813—Provincial representatives form a congress, abolish slavery, and create office of supreme director to rule Argentina

1814—José de San Martín becomes Argentine army commander

1816—Congress meets at San Miguel de Tucumán, declares independence under name of United Provinces of the Río de la Plata

1817—San Martín defeats Spanish at Chacabuco

1818—San Martín completes military takeover of Chile

1819—Centralist constitution defeated

1820—Argentine government claims Malvinas

1825-1828—Argentina at war with Brazil; Uruguay set up as a buffer state between the two countries

1828-1829—Argentine civil war

1829—Juan Manuel de Rosas elected governor of Buenos Aires

1833—British retake Malvinas (Falkland Islands)

1838-1840—Troubles with France; Buenos Aires blockaded

1845-1848—Troubles with France and England; Buenos Aires again blockaded

1852-1861—Civil war between Buenos Aires and provinces

1853—Constitution approved

1862—Buenos Aires declared Argentine capital

1865-1870—War of the Triple Alliance against Paraguay

1874-1880—Conquest of the desert; Indians defeated

1880-1886—Continued expansion of frontier; railroad building increases; meat packing becomes major business

1890—Economic depression

1916—World War I; Argentina declares neutrality

1922—Yaciminetos Petroliferos Fiscales (YPF) formed to help discover oil in Argentina

1929-1930—Worldwide depression; Argentina hit hard

1930—Military under General José F. Uriburu takes control of the government

1932-1938—Argentina begins slow economic recovery

1936—Carlos Saavedra Lamas receives Nobel Peace Prize

1939—World War II starts; Argentina supposedly neutral, but military supports Nazis in Germany and Fascists in Italy

1943—President Ramón S. Castillo declares state of siege; military coup

1944—Juan Domingo Perón named vice-president

1945—Argentina declares war on Germany and Japan; civilian rioters object to military government; Perón forced to resign and is placed under arrest, but returns to be nominated for presidency

1946-1955—Perón is president of Argentina; economic difficulties increase; Peronist party formed; constitution of 1949 replaces constitution of 1853; newspapers closed; military revolt put down; Eva Perón dies (1952); conflict with Roman Catholic church

1947—Physiologist Bernardo Houssay receives Nobel Prize

1955—Military coup overthrows Perón

1958-1962—Reform administration of Arturo Frondizi

1962—Military coup overthrows Frondizi

1963—Navy revolt crushed by army

1964—Perón attempts to return to Argentina from Spain but is prevented from entering the country

1966 — Military coup overthrows President Arturo Illía; Congress dissolved

1968-1969 — Riots and strikes rock Argentina; army revolt put down

1970 — Former President Pedro Eugenio Aramburu kidnapped and killed by terrorists; thousands arrested; Luis Federico Leloir receives Nobel Prize in chemistry

1973 — Perón returns to Argentina and is reelected president

1974 — Perón dies; Maria Estela (Isabel) Martínez de Perón named president; military coup deposes Señora Perón

1976 — The military, led by Lieutenant General Jorge Videla, takes control

1978 — Argentina wins World Championship in soccer

1979 — Argentina wins Junior World Championship in soccer

1980 — Nobel Peace Prize awarded to Adolfo Pérez Esquivel

1982 — Argentina at war with Britain over the Malvinas Islands; British retain control of the islands; President Leopoldo Galtieri deposed and replaced by General Reynaldo Benito Antonio Bignone

1982-1983 — General strikes protesting low wages and government corruption

1983 — Dr. Raúl Alfonsín becomes the first civilian president since the 1976 coup

1987 — Treasury secretary Mario Brodersohn threatens to stop payment on Argentina's $53 billion foreign debt

1988 — Pope John Paul II visits Argentina; more than one million attend as he presides over the first Palm Sunday mass outside of Rome since the Middle Ages

1989 — Carlos Saul Menem is sworn in as president during the worst economic crisis in Argentine history, with plans to transform the country's economy

1992 — The government returns to the peso

1993 — Menem unveils a short-term economic plan centered on promoting growth for manufacturing companies and farmers, creating a million jobs, and reducing the inflation rate to 4 percent; the law providing for censorship of the press is repealed

1994 — The World Bank approves $508.5 million in loans to fund banking loans to small businesses; 9,000 sheep and cattle are killed to prevent spread of the worst outbreak of hoof and mouth disease in two decades; the U.S. sells 36 warplanes to rebuild the Argentine airforce under Argentina's intention to settle international disputes by nonmilitary means

IMPORTANT PEOPLE

Luis Agote (1868-1954), professor of clinical medicine who discovered first practical method to transfuse blood without it coagulating (hardening)

Juan Bautista Alberdi (1810-1884), political philosopher and "father of the Argentine constitution"

Amancio Alcorta (1805-1862), first native Argentine composer

Juan Bautista Ambrosetti (1865-1917), archaeologist and folk music specialist

Florentino Ameghino (1854-1911), anthropologist

Hilario Ascásubi (1807-1875), poet who praised the gaucho life-style as symbolic of freedom

Martín del Barco Centenera (1536-1605), Spanish-born priest who wrote epic poetry about Argentina; first author to use the word *Argentina* to describe the country

Liliana Belfiore (1952-   ), ballerina

Arturo Beruti (1862-1938), composer whose *The White Cat* was one of the first Argentine operas to be well received on European stages

Carlos Bielicki, world champion juvenile chess champion (1957)

Jorge Luis Borges (1899-1986), short-story author, essayist, and poet; considered the greatest contemporary Spanish poet

Estanislao del Campo (1834-1880), poet

Juan Díaz de Solís (1470?-1516), discoverer of Argentina

Adolfo Pérez Esquivel, winner of Nobel Peace Prize in 1980

Juan Manuel Fangio (1911-   ), five-time world champion auto racer

Rene Favaloro, heart specialist

Luis Angel Firpo (?-1960), boxing champion nicknamed "Wild Bull of the Pampas"

Victor Galíndez, world middleweight boxing champion (1974-1979)

Enrique García Velloso, dramatist who wrote *Jesus Nazareno,* one of the best plays in modern Argentine history

José Hernández (1834-1886), poet and journalist whose poem *Martin Fierro* was considered the best of the gaucho-revolutionary works. His writings have been translated into fifty-four languages.

Bernardo Houssay (1887-1971), physiologist who won the Nobel Prize in 1947

Carlos Saavedra Lamas (?-1959), winner of Nobel Peace Prize in 1936

Manuel de Lavarden, nineteenth-century playwright who wrote *Siripo,* considered the beginning of theatrical life in Argentina

Luis Federico Leloir (1906-   ), chemist who won the Nobel Prize in 1970

Domingo Liotta, cardiologist who invented the bypass valve to replace the left ventricle of the heart

Leopoldo Lugones (1874-1938), author of "La Guerra Gaucho," "Golden Mountains," and other works that have greatly influenced other Spanish-speaking poets

Martha Lynch, comtemporary author

Salvador Mazza (1886-1946), bacteriologist

Pedro de Mendoza (1487-1537), Spanish explorer who built first fort at Buenos Aires

César Luis Menotti, soccer star

Antonia Mercé (1888?-1936), ballerina who originated neoclassical style of Spanish dance, danced under name of *Argentinita*

Carlos Monzón, world middleweight boxing champion (1970-77)

Francisco Moreno, nineteenth-century explorer and mapmaker

Jorge Newbery, aviation pioneer

Rafael Obligado (1851-1920), poet

Victoria Ocampo, Argentine publisher

José Leon Pagano (1875-1964), painter whose *Old Tuscan Woman* masterpiece was among the first internationally recognized Argentine work of art

Roberto Payro (1867-1928), actor

Pascual Pérez, flyweight boxing champion of the world (1954-59)

Juan Domingo Perón (1895-1974), president of Argentina (1946-55 and 1973-74)

Astor Piazolla, contemporary musician and master of the *bandoncon,* an accordionlike instrument used for accompanying the tango

Prilidiano Pueyrredón (1823-70), painter

Bernardino Rivadivia (1780-1845), first president of the United Provinces of La Plata (1826-27)

Juan Manuel de Rosas (1793-1877), governor and captain-general of the province of Buenos Aires (1829-32 and 1835-52)

Ernesto Sábato, contemporary novelist

José de San Martín (1778-1850), revolutionary general who led Argentine army to victory over the Spanish

Domingo Faustino Sarmiento (1811-88), president of Argentina from 1868-74, proponent of education

Eduardo Sivori (1847-1918), painter who helped found the Association for Development of Fine Arts

Raul Soldi (1905-   ), contemporary artist

Luis de Tejeda (1604-?), first native Argentine poet

Alberto Vaccarezz, contemporary playwright

Juan Vucetich, invented technique of fingerprinting

PRESIDENTS OF ARGENTINA

Bernardino Rivadavia	(1826-1827)
Vicente López y Planes	(1827-1828)
Juan Manuel de Rosas	(1829-1833, 1835-1852)
Justo José de Urquiza	(1854-1860)
Santiago Derqui	(1860-1862)
Bartolomé Mitre	(1862-1868)
Domingo Faustino Sarmiento	(1868-1874)
Nicola Avellenda	(1874-1880)
Julio A. Roca	(1880-1886)
Miguel Juárez Celman	(1886-1890)
Carlos Pellegrini	(1890-1892)
Luis Sáenz Peña	(1892-1895)
José Evaristo Uriburu	(1895-1898)
Julio A. Roca	(1898-1904)
Manuel Quintana	(1904-1906)
José Figueroa Alcorta	(1906-1910)
Roque Sáenz Peña	(1910-1914)
Victorino de la Plaza	(1914-1916)
Hipólito Irigoyen	(1916-1922)
Marcelo Torcuato de Alvear	(1922-1928)
Hipólito Irigoyen	(1928-1930)
José Felix Uriburu	(1930-1932)
Agustín P. Justo	(1932-1938)
Roberto M. Ortiz	(1938-1941)
Ramón S. Castillo	(1941-1943)
Arturo Rawson	(1943)
Pedro Pablo Ramírez	(1943-1944)
Edelmiro J. Fárrell	(1944-1946)
Juan Domingo Perón	(1946-1955)
Eduardo Lonardi	(1955)
Pedro Eugenio Aramburu	(1955-1958)
Arturo Frondizi	(1958-1962)
José María Guido	(1962-1963)
Arturo U. Illia	(1963-1966)
Juan Carlos Onganía	(1966-1970)
Roberto M. Levingstone	(1970-1971)
Alejandro Lanusse	(1971-1973)
Hector José Cámpora	(1973)
Juan Domingo Perón	(1973-1974)
Maria Estela (Isabel) Martínez de Perón	(1974-1976)
military junta	(1976-1978)
General Jorge Videla	(1978-1981)
General Roberto Viola	(1981)
General Leopoldo Galtieri	(1981-1982)
General Reynaldo Benito Antonio Bignone	(1982-1983)
Dr. Raúl Alfonsín	(1983-1989)
Carlos Saul Menem	(1989-)

INDEX

Page numbers that appear in boldface type indicate illustrations

About the Author

Martin Hintz, a former newspaper reporter, has written more than a dozen books for young people. The subjects range from training elephants to other social studies titles included in the Childrens Press Enchantment of the World series. He and his family currently live in Milwaukee, Wisconsin. Hintz has a master's degree in journalism and is a professional travel writer/photographer who has won numerous awards for his work.